DICTIONARY OF E-COMMERCE

DICTIONARY OF E-COMMERCE

Compiled & Edited by

J. ERIKSON

ANMOL PUBLICATIONS PVT. LTD.
NEW DELHI-110 002 (INDIA)

ANMOL PUBLICATIONS PVT. LTD.
4374/4B, Ansari Road, Daryaganj
New Delhi-110 002
Phones: 23261597, 23278000, 23255577
Email: anmolpublications@vsnl.com

Dictionary of E-Commerce

First Edition 2003
ISBN 81-261-1460-6

PRINTED IN INDIA

Published by J.L. Kumar for Anmol Publications Pvt. Ltd., New Delhi-110 002 and Printed at Mehra Offset Press, Delhi.

PROLOGUE

Electronic Commerce popularly called E-Commerce is often used interchangeably with the term "E-Business". In reality, E-business carries a much broader sense rather than just the shopping. Some people also use the term "Internet Commerce" to mean electronic commerce that specifically uses the Internet or the web for data transmission. In its simplest form, it refers to shopping on the part of the Internet called the World Wide Web or the Web. But web shopping is only a small part of the E-Commerce picture. The term also includes online stock transactions, downloading software without going near a store, etc. For most businesses, it's not really about selling at all but about improving relationships among suppliers, distributors and customers. Electronic Commerce can be defined as any form of computerised buying and selling, both by consumers and from company to company, which facilitates choosing the goods, ordering, delivery, after sales support and payment.

E-Commerce is shrinking the world. Distant markets suddenly are within easy reach, saving business time and money, prospecting and presenting new business opportunities based on better and more thorough information. A company that incorporates electronic commerce as a major component of its marketing strategy stays at least in line with, if not ahead, of the competition.

What really pushes a business organization to move to a paperless environment? There can be numerous reasons to place the organization on the e-commerce bandwagon. Although these reasons are specific to every organization but some of the common ones are:

Competition – The organization is either forced by the competition or it can pre-empt the competition by moving ahead of others in joining e-commerce. An excellent example is Dell Computers that was the first to start sale of computers through the Internet thereby reducing cost. It also provided a facility to the customers to assemble the computer choosing different hardware components such as Memory, Hard Disk, CD Drive, Monitor, etc. IBM, Compaq and other manufacturer's had to change their marketing strategy to find ways to reduce operational costs by adopting the e-business model of sale through Internet.

Global Reach – The Internet has crashed the geographical boundaries and the entire world has shrieked to a global village. This permits the customers to make purchases from any part of the world without actually visiting the place. This widens the reach of the companies to the entire globe. This further translates into 24 hour, seven days a week and 365 days in a year business for the company. For example, books can be purchased from *amazon.com* from any part of the world, AT&T allows the customer to receive the bill and authorise payment electronically from any part of the world.

Customer Service – Personalised and Customised services through Internet is one of the greatest advantages e-commerce offers. The customers can customise the product according to their own taste such as: online newspaper. The customers can be updated on the status of order placed by them when it goes through various stages of processing such as packing, shipping, etc. Pre-sale and Post-sale support are an important ingredient of the e-commerce package.

Value Addition - A product has to go through various stages of value addition from manufacturers to the consumers and at each stage the cost is added up making the product expensive for the consumer. This business chain can be shortened through the adoption of e-commerce thereby making the product cheaply available to the consumers.

Nettish Products – The products which are more suitable for purchase through the Internet as their delivery takes place through the Net are referred to as Nettish Products, e.g. E-mail, E-Greetings, Software, Chat Software, etc.

The fall in operational costs, higher quality, integration of supply and distribution chain, improvements in efficiency levels and etc. are too attractive for any business to ignore. Business is increasing on the Internet because it provides cost-effective alternative.

The advantages of e-commerce for business-to-business are: Lower purchasing costs, Reduced Inventory Control, Lower cycle time, Efficient customer service, Lower sales and marketing costs, New Markets (Sales opportunities), Smooth business operations and, Reduced Document processing costs.

Some of the cost-effective uses of e-commerce are: Marketing, Advertising, Sales, Business Communication and Brand Equity.

Keeping in view the rapidly growing importance of e-commerce, the present dictionary is prepared. The terms are judiciously selected and defined accurately and explained. Substantially based on authoritative sources, this can be used as a dependable reference tool.

I am thankful to all the scholars and experts whose definitions/explanations are liberally borrowed here. I hope this dictionary will prove useful and informative to one and all.

—J. Erikson

AAA server. A server that provides authentication, authorization, and accounting security services. Standards for such servers include RADIUS and TACACS+.

above the fold. The top portion of a Web page which can be seen without scrolling. The term is adopted from newspapers where it refers to the top half of the front page.

acceptable use policy. A policy established for a computing resource (e.g. a Web site) that describes how users may access and use the facility. Among other issues, an acceptable use policy typically addresses who may use the resource, the purposes for which the resource may be used, how much of the resource (memory, computing capacity) may be used, copying and publication of content, security requirements, and privacy requirements.

accessibility. State or quality of Web sites being accessible to users with disabilities.

access profile. The information maintained by an AAA server for each user. It includes information needed for authentication and accounting. It also specifies the user's access privileges for authorization by the AAA server.

access URL. A URL used by a payment switch to enable delivery of a purchased product. The access URL contains the name of the server which can provide the product, the identification of the product, an identification of the buyer (e.g. the buyer's IP address), an expiration date for the access URL, and a digital signature for the access URL.

account. An area partitioned for a user of a particular host computer. To assure validity, account holders cannot gain access without using assigned login and password information.

ACL. (**A**ccess **C**ontrol **L**ist) A list of resources and the usernames of people who are permitted access to those resources within a computer system.

acquirer. Financial institution that maintains the merchant card processing services and receives transactions to be distributed to the card issuers for a merchant.

active content. Programs that are embedded transparently in Web pages that cause some type of action to occur.

active attack. An attempt to break security by altering information. An active attack may or may not require decrypting the information attacked. See passive attack and replay attack.

activeX. An object, or control, that contains programs and properties that are put into Web pages to perform particular tasks.

ad. See advertisement.

ad auction. A service that allows Web publishers to sell previously unsold ad space at the last minute for whatever the market will bear. Advertisers are able to buy space at exceptionally low cost-per-thousand. See advertisement.

ad audience. Number of unique users exposed to an ad within a specified time period.

ad blockers. Software on a user's browser which prevents banner and interactive ads from being displayed.

ADC. Automatic Data Capture. The general capability of gathering status, location, and identifying information without human intervention. ADC reduces the need for manually keying in data and the risk of inaccuracies. Technologies used in ADC include bar coding, magnetic stripes, smart cards, machine vision, biometric identification, voice recognition, optical character recognition, and Radio Frequency Identification.

ad centric measurement. Audience measurement derived from a third party ad server's own server logs.

ad copy. Printed text in an advertisement.

address. An individualized name (or number) identifying a computer user or computer. Used in network communications for the transmission of messages for a particular person or machine.

address locator. A type of service available from a number of Web sites that provides the addresses and phone numbers of individuals and businesses input by the user.

add URL/site/page. Refers to getting your site indexed by search engines and Web site directories, so that people can find your site. Same as search engine submissions.

Address Verification Service (AVS). Service in which a merchant can verify a credit card holder's address with the Issuing Bank. Required by VISA for credit card processing over the Web.

ad impression/view. Single display of an ad that is viewed by a Web user on a Web page, in a newsletter or e-mail.

ad inventory. All the advertising space available for sale on a given Web site. See advertisement.

adjustment. Debit or credit to a credit card holder or merchant account to correct a transaction error.

ad management service bureau. A company that serves Web publishers by delivering advertisements (See ad serving system) on the publisher's Web site and reporting on the ads that were served (See impressions) and how many times user's clicked on them (See click-through rate). Also see third-party ad management.

ad network. A company that contracts with a number of Web sites to sell advertising space on the sites. See advertisement and run of network.

ADO. (ActiveX Data Objects). See activeX.

ad request. The request to an ad server to display an advertisement within a Web page. For many possible reasons the ad may fail to display. See ad serving system.

ad rotation. Number of banner ads that are rotated into an ad space on a Web site by software residing on a site's server, or a remotely hosted ad server facility.

ad serving system. A system which inserts ads (usually banners) into Web pages when the pages are accessed by a user. The Web page and the ad may be served (i.e. delivered) by entirely different companies using geographically separated servers. The system requires that the designated Web pages have links embedded in them that correspond to certain sizes of ads and to certain categories of products or services. Often the company delivering the Web page receives compensation for attracting users who view the advertising but has little or no control or interest in the specific advertising messages delivered. Often the company operating the ad serving system is not advertising any of its own products or services but is acting as a middleman between the advertiser and the company that supplies the Web pages. See impression.

ADSL. Asymmetric Digital Subscriber Line. A technology for providing high transmissions speeds for video and voice to homes over ordinary copper telephone wire. It will be most cost- effective in areas with low market penetration of "cable" TV. In areas with higher penetration coax is expected to be more cost-effective.

ad space. Space on a Web page that is reserved for advertisements.

advertisement. A message from a company (the advertiser) to potential customers that attempts to influence or reinforce the customers' attitudes and/or behavior toward purchasing the advertiser's products or services, or towards obtaining more information, including further marketing messages, from the advertiser. Advertising is usually not requested by the user but is embedded within information or entertainment that the user has chosen to see or listen to. Traditional media for delivering advertising include newspapers, magazines, television, and radio. On the Internet, advertising is most commonly delivered by E-mail or in the form of banners embedded in Web pages. Advertisers almost always pay the media or content providers for "space" or "placement" within the content that attracts customers.

advertising. The planning for, development of, and placement of advertisements. Also, the set of advertisements placed by a merchant in a given campaign.

advertising network. Advertising network refers to an infomediary, which serves between a group (network) of web sites (which want to host advertisements) and advertisers which want to run advertisements on those sites. DoubleClick is the most well known advertising network. It can serve advertisements on any of its member sites, and can mine data from users who interact with those sites in order to serve more appropriate advertisements. An advertiser can buy a run of network package, or a run of category package within the network. The advertising network serves advertisements from its ad server, which responds to a site once a page is called. A snipet of code is called from the ad server, that represents the advertising banner.

advertorial. An advertisement that appears to be editorial content. In printed media advertorials are generally labeled as advertising but on the Web their purpose is often disguised.

ad view. A page view of a Web page that contains an advertisement.

Advisory Commission on Electronic Commerce. A group set up by the U.S. Congress under the Internet Tax Freedom Act of 1998 to recommend a plan for taxing sales made over the Internet.

AEI. Automatic Equipment Identification. The general capability of identifying movable equipment without human intervention.

affiliate directories. Categorized indexes of affiliate programs.

affiliate fraud. Bogus or unlawful activity generated by an affiliate in an attempt to make money.

affiliate marketing. Use of affiliates to help market a Web site's products and services in return for a payment for each sale, lead, action, or visitor generated.

affiliate merchants. Advertisers in an affiliate marketing relationship.

affiliate networks. Online advertising agencies that sells ad space on behalf of its network of affiliate sites. Affiliates are paid on a per click, lead, registration, or sale basis.

affiliate program. An affiliate program is a form of advertising, on the web, that rewards the affiliates (self-selected advertisers) for driving traffic to the advertiser (CTR) or for subsequent transactions (CPA). An affiliate program uses a multi-level marketing concept where consumers (affiliates) attract additional consumers. Some affiliate programs are multi-tiered, thus increasing the income earning opportunities for the affiliates (rewarded for their traffic and the traffic of affiliates they recruit). Marketers have the option of developing their own in-house affiliate program (Amazon.com and bn.com are examples) or joining one or more of the large affiliate networks (Beefree, Linkshare or CommissionJunction). Affiliates have the potential to earn significant money, if done correctly. This book store is the author's example of an Amazon affiliate. Marketing vehicles may sign up for an affiliate program to use its excess advertising inventory (unsold banners).

affiliates. Publishers who is a member of an affiliate program or network.

affiliate software. Software used by affiliate managers to track and report activity (clicks, leads, registration, sales) generated by its affiliates.

affinity card. A type of credit card, first marketed in 1985, which ties into a special consumer interest. Affinity cards include product benefit cards which provide bonuses for usage, lifestyle cards which usually contribute a portion of each transaction to a specific charity, and personality cards which feature images on the card associated with a particular celebrity.

agent. A program that performs information gathering, information filtering, and/or mediation on behalf of a person or entity.

AH. See IP authentication header.

Ah-Ha. A popular pay per click search engine used by 10,000 advertisers and processes some 120 million searches a month.

AllTheWeb. The testing domain for the "FAST" search engine.

Alpha/Beta. The terms alpha and beta refer to releases of software that are typically not ready for commercial use. Alpha refers to the very early release, which is typically very buggy and only released to few people internal to the organization. It is helpful, in development, to get feedback very quickly from the hacker community, or potential customers with the beta version. Releasing a beta version has become standard practice with the evolution of the internet as a mode of distribution for the software. It is a part of the development model for open source software.

alphanumeric rankings. Alphanumeric rankings are used by Web site directories to rank its listings. The listings are displayed in the order of the ASCII character set (punctuation marks, mathematical and other conventional symbols, numbers, then letters).

AltaVista. A popular search engine and claims to be the first searchable full-text database of the World Wide Web back in December, 1995.

alternate text. Alternative text description of an image for users who disable image downloading in their browser. Also appears as a pop-up text message when a user moves their mouse over an image.

animated GIF. GIF graphic that rotates through a series of static images to create the effect of animation.

Anonymizers. Intermediaries which prevent Web sites from seeing a user's IP (Internet Protocol) address. Every computer connected to the Internet has an IP address.

anonymous electronic cash. Electronic cash that cannot be traced back to the person who spent it.

anonymous FTP. File Transfer Protocol allows you to connect to a site, search through available files, and download any file, document, or program without having to establish a user-id and password on the system where the material resides. By using the special user-id "anonymous", the network user will circumvent local security checks and have access to publicly accessible files on the remote system. Most systems that permit anonymous login require the user's e-mail address as the password.

antialiasing. Smoothing of text, or an image, to remove rough sharp edges.

ANSI (American National Standards Institute). The coordinating body for electrical, mechanical, and other technical standards in the United States.

AOL Search. A search portal which everyone - not just AOL Internet access subscribers - with access to the Internet can use.

Apache. Apache is the name of the project team which created the Apache Web server, a freely available Web serving program.

API. API refers to Application Programming Interface. It is the interface that gives program developers access to develop programs that work on a particular platform. Thus for Microsoft's Windows platform, the API is win32. To develop a program to run on the windows platform, you must write to the win32 API, thus the win32 API is the software developer's platform for windows. By encouraging other software programmers to develop to your platform, you are able to encourage lock-in as more people become dependent on the platform. A key stratgeic issue for a software company is whether to develop a developer's community, which builds software to its platform, or whether to keep the development internal to the organization.

applets. Small programs embedded in a Web page that gives special functionality, usually written in Java.

application. Software that executes a particular task, such as word processing or spreadsheet analysis.

application-centric EDI. An update to traditional electronic data interchange (EDI) that uses secure transmission methods to facilitate the exchange of information between secure applications, typically residing at different companies (e.g. vendor and customer). Deployment of such secured applications over their intranets and Internets is faster, less costly, and more effective than traditional EDI. See electronic data interchange, information security, transmission, application, intranet, and Internet in the hard copy dictionary.

Application Service Provider (ASP). A company that hosts an application and data for one or more customers, providing the hardware, software, infrastructure, and basic maintenance. The provider supports remote access to the application by the customer, usually over the Internet. The provider usually has expertise in the specific application hosted and may provide enhancements to it. Advantages to the customer, versus running the application in-house, include guaranteed performance, a robust data center, in-depth support from a skilled staff, and better economics.

Archie. A program used to search files at FTP sites; there are currently about 30 Archie servers in the world.

architect(ure). Architecture refers to the planning phase of the software development process, much like architecture refers to the same in the process of building a house. The builders are the coders of the product, once it is architected. This is an extraordinarily important phase of the overall development of the product, and consists of thoroughly understanding and articulating the needs of the users (of the system) and the coders (for the system). This serves as a roadmap for current and future development for the product. Poor architecture may not be apparent during early releases of the product (the alpha and beta phases), but as the product evolves, architectural decisions will become more impactful to development.

ArchitextSpider. The name given to Excite's search engine spider, when it used to crawl the Web indexing Web pages.

archive. Single file containing a collection of compressed, or zipped, files for efficient storage. To extract the original files from the compressed file, you use an unzipping program, such as PKZIP, StuffIt Expander, tar, or WinZip.

archive site. A mechanism that renders access to a collection of files across the Internet; also, a computer on which such a collection is stored.

archiving. Saving a log on a storage device.

ARPAnet (Advanced Research Projects Agency). The experimental network, established in the 1970s, where the theories and software on which the Internet is based were tested.

ASCII (American Standard Code for Information Exchange). The standard method for encoding characters as 8-bit sequences of binary numbers, allowing a maximum of

256 characters. Text files are customarily called "ASCII files".

ASDL (Asymmetric Digital Subscriber Line). Internet connections using DSL protocol with bandwidths from 16 to 640 Kbps upstream and 1.5 to 9 Mbps downstream. See bandwidth.

ask an expert. Sites that have experts in different fields offering answers to posted questions. While some ask an expert sites are free, others charge on a per question e-mailed, or per minute of advice given basis.

Ask Jeeves. A unique search engine that combines a knowledge base of answers to roughly 7 million commonly asked questions.

ASP (Application Service Provider). Company that offers individuals or enterprises access over the Internet to software applications and related services that would otherwise have to be located on their own personal or enterprise computers.

associations. Organization which administers and promotes different types of credit cards that are licensing and regulatory agencies for bankcard activities.

asynchronous/synchronous communication: Direct communication, where all parties involved in the communication are present at the same time (an event) is a form of synchronous communication. Examples include a telephone conversation, a company board meeting a chat room event and instant messaging. Asynchronous communication does not require that all parties involved in the communication need to be present and available at the same time. Examples of this include e-mail (the receiver does not have to be logged on when the sender sends the e-mail message), discussion boards, which allow conversations to evolve and community to develop over a period of time, and text messaging over cell phones.

ATM (Asynchronous Transfer Mode). Internet connections with bandwidths of up to 622 Gbps. See bandwidth.

attachments. Computer files electronically attached to an e-mail and sent along with it.

auction pricing system: Using an auction pricing system, sellers are not constrained by having to fix a price without knowing what the market will bare (traditional pricing methodology). If a seller sets a price too low, using a classified advertisement for example, the demand will be high and the product will be purchased. The seller, however, will not get the most revenue the market would have paid, if the buyers had had to compete for the purchase. The buyer who wanted the product most (willing to pay the highest price) would not automatically receive the product. Conversely, if the seller advertises too high a price, using a classified adversitement, the product will not sell. By allowing buyers to bid up the price from a low price point, the product will sell to the highest bidder (assuming it clears a minimum asking price). The auction pricing system is a dynamic pricing model, much like the reverse pricing model. Game Theory can impact the strategies involved in setting a starting price (for the seller) and bidding strategies for the buyers. Examples include: Ebay and QXL.com.

audit trail. Information on the significant steps in the progress of a transaction which allows an auditor to determine that there are no errors in the reporting of the transaction. In electronic commerce a good audit trail can help resolve programming errors and discrepancies in the how a transaction is recorded by the parties to the transaction.

authentication. The process of identifying users before they are allowed access to computer systems or networks, typically by user-ids and passwords. Technique that limits Internet or intranet access to those visitors who identify themselves by entering a username or password.

authorization. Approval of a credit card transaction by a card-issuing bank or approved service provider for a specific sum of money. The authorization indicates that the credit card holder has enough credit to be able to make the purchase.

automated crime. The use of a software program to invade a system, commit a crime (e.g. illegal transfer of funds) and erase all traces of the crime, usually within a small fraction of a second.

automated fuel terminal (AFT). Allows purchasers of gasoline to "pay at the pump" with a thermal printer installed at every pump.

Autoresponder: Autoresponders are used to send an automatic e-mail in response to an incoming e-mail message. This allows for the sender to know the e-mail has been received, which is important due to the asynchronous nature of the medium. They are often used by company employees to alert people they are away on vacation, thus delaying a potential response. They can also be used effectively in customer service by indicating to the consumer:

— The query was received
— Other alternate means to find information
— A response timeframe
— Additional marketing material

Note: In some cases, an autoresponder can be used to distribute a digital product, as a response to an e-mail request.

average costs. The average cost of a unit of product is made up of its fixed costs/#units produced, and the variable cost per unit. With digital products, where the variable costs are very small (and in some instances zero) the average cost of the product declines as more units are produced and sold. Thus the market leader for a product typically has the lowest average costs per unit. This allows the leader to have increased margins, and increased flexibility to lower price. This is one of the reasons why first-mover advantage can be so important.

B2B/BtoB (Business-to-Business). Trade between businesses rather than between businesses and consumers.

B2C: B2C refers to business-to-consumer trade, retail trade. Similarly B2B refers to business-to-business, distribution channel (value chain). C2B refers to consumer-to-business, and uses a reverse pricing model. C2C refers to consumer-to-consumer, an auction-style model.

B2G/BtoG (Business-to-Government). Trade between businesses and government.

B-ISDN. A very high speed data communications service that supports rates of 1.5 million bits per second over fiber-optic telephone lines.

backbone. A high-speed connection within a network that links shorter (usually slower) branch circuits. An example is the NSFNet, generally considered to be the backbone of the Internet in the United States.

back-end. Application or program that serves indirectly in support of the front-end services. For example, a CGI search script is a back-end application that processes and returns results for a search form submission.

bandwidth. Measure in kilobytes of the traffic transferred via one of the several Internet protocols. The amount of data that can be transmitted in a fixed amount of time. Also, the number of simultaneous site visitors that a Web site can accommodate without degrading service.

bandwidth transfer. The amount of data your Web hosting plan allows you to transfer in a given month. 'Transfer' means any data that needs to be sent to visitors at a site, such as HTML pages, images, sounds, music, and other files you have available for download.

bank cards. Debit or credit cards issued by a bank or financial institution.

(advertising) banners. Banners are the primary form of advertisements on the web. The standard banner usually appears at the top of a web page, and will link to a target web page, that may be the homepage of the advertiser or a target page developed by the advertiser that is more directly relevant to the message of the banner (a better use). Web advertising can also come in the form of buttons (smaller, usually in the left hand column), interstitial pages, pop-up pages or text advertisements. The IAB has developed banner size standards.

banner exchange. A banner exchange program is a program designed to allow marketers to exchange banners (a form of bartering) to enable marketers to promote their sites without the outlay of cash. A program typically allows a marketer to display one advertisement, across the network, for every two advertisements it hosts on its site. Unlike a straight exchange with one entity, exchange programs allow for the possibility for the banner to be displayed on many web sites (those sites that participate in that particular network). The Free Banner Exchange Megalist is a good resource for identifying these exchanges.

barrier(s) to entry. Barrier to Entry refers to the costs incurred for a new entrant to enter a marketplace. Examples include fixed costs such as the development of a factory (for traditional manufactured goods), branding and lock-in established by current competitors in the form of switching costs. Barriers to entry can also refer to any "hidden" cost established to reduce freedom of choice. Thus traditional retailing environments, that rely on geography as a competitive advantage, are building barriers to entry to those not in close proximity to their customer base.

barter. Bartering is the trade of goods from one enterprise to another, without the transfer of payments. Many internet businesses are trading their products and services, to avoid payments and / or to stimulate demand, at the early stages of their life cycle. This has also become common practice for the trade of banner advertisements. Banner exchange programs enable small advertisers to exchange advertising space, but large enterprises are also involved in this practice.

Bartering was the means of exchange between traders and customers in markets, before money was developed, so is closely associated with very early market development! In the early model, money was developed to make markets more liquid, with the internet, bartering is used due to the lack of liquidity of many internet businesses.

batch. A full day's worth of transactions collected together ready to be processed by a credit card processor.

baud rate. (Same as *bps*—Bits Per Second). A unit used to measure the number of data bits a modem can transfer in one second. One baud is how many signals a modem can handle in one second. Information is measured in bits, and bits come in the signal. Higher baud modems can send and receive more signals in a second, and the faster speeds also cram more bits into a signal.

Bay9. Bay9, formerly known as Rocketlinks, now known as Xuppa, is a popular pay per click search engine processing some 125 million page views a month.

BBS (Bulletin Board System). Computers access by remote users via modems for discussion, file downloads, and other BBS services. BBSs are typically stand-alone systems not on the Internet, though many have gateways.

BCC (Blind Carbon Copy). Insert email addresses into the BCC field of an outgoing email to send an email to one or more recipients, without revealing the email addresses of all the recipients.

beacon. Code placed in an ad on a Web page, or in an email, to track whether the ad was delivered correctly.

beta software. Software that has been developed to the point where it can be tested for reliability and usability in customer environments but not to the point where it can be broadly sold, used, or supported. Beta sites are customer sites where the software is tested.

beyond the banner. Every other form of Internet advertising, except the standard animated GIF banners. For example, interstitials, which are pages inserted in between Web pages for the purpose of advertising or brand reinforcement.

bill presentment. The delivery of a bill or invoice to a client or customer for payment. Third party specialists compete with banks to provide electronic bill presentment over the Internet, especially for companies that serve large numbers of consumers (i.e. utility companies).

binary file. Refers to a file that contains information in a non-text form (graphics, sounds, spreadsheets, etc.). Any file that is not a text file. Any arrangements of bits that is meaningful to a computer, without regard to any correspondence to a human-readable character set.

bit. Short for binary digit. The smallest unit of data in a computer. A bit has a single boolean value, either 0 or 1.

BITNET. An acronym for "Because It's Time Network", a cooperative education and research network.

Blackbird. A multimedia authoring tool analogous to HTML. Blackbird was developed by Microsoft for developing content to be published on the Microsoft Network (MSN). It includes Standard Generalized Markup Language (SGML) and Object Linking and Embedding Technology (OLE) controls called OCXes. Helper applications developed by other companies can be linked to Blackbird using OCXes to present 3-D displays, editable spreadsheets, animation and other capabilities.

blind certificate. A digital certificate which does not contain the name or other identifying information about the user to whom it is issued. Such a certificate can be used to verify some limited information about the user or to associate a user with a series of communications or transactions without revealing the identity of the user. Applications include revocable cash transactions and ongoing anonymous communications over the network.

blog, blogger. A blogger is someone who publishes a Web log (or "blog"), an online, very public, theme-specific record intended for the Web savvy reader. The article My blog, my self explains this trend recently embraced by people from all walks of life to record their daily thoughts and share them with the world. According to Jennifer Balderama, CNET News.com's copy chief and publisher of the Web log Nonsense Verse:

"Web logs give voice to people whom just a decade ago, you never would have heard from. There are war blogs, peace blogs, food blogs, crude blogs, humor blogs, culture blogs to occupy your day. Geek blogs, freak blogs, teen blogs, mean blogs, fanaticals and radicals who like to rant away. Worker bees and histories, punditry and poetry, diversity, adversity and spicy verbal play. Optimists, pessimists, enthusiasts and hobbyists, journalists and journal-ists with something big to say." BTW, you can create your own blog at blogger.com.

bonus impressions. Free ad impressions above the commitments outlined in the approved insertion order.

booked space. Number of sold ad impressions for an ad space.

bookmark (or favorite). Most Web browsers give you an option of adding a URL to a "HotList" or by marking it with a "bookmark". By doing this, you can store the linking information (the URL) to any Web pages you plan to revisit. That way, if you decide to go back to a Web site, its URL is already catalogued and at your fingertips for easy reference. (Spry Mosaic uses "hotlists", Netscape Navigator uses "bookmarks" and Microsoft Internet Explorer uses "favorites"). Other Web browsers may use those terms, or may call their URL-saving feature something else.)

Boolean logic. A system for searching and retrieving information from computers by using and combining terms such as AND, OR, and NOT to sort data.

bot. Synonymous with spider, which is the first part of a search engine. It automatically and frequently searches the Web to find pages and updates its database of information about old Web sites.

(shopping) bots: Bots are software programs developed to help the user search the web to identify and compare products for purchase. Examples include: DealPilot.com, FrictionLess.com, and Epinions.com. They are also referred to as intelligent agents.

bounce. When email cannot be delivered and is returned to the sending mail server.

bps (Bits Per Second). Refers to the speed at which a particular modem can transmit data. Divide the bits per second by 10 to get an approximate idea of how many characters per second a modem is transmitting data.

brand. A name or symbol chosen by a company to uniquely identify a set of products and/or services that the company has established or hopes to establish in the minds of its customers as an indication of certain levels of quality and trustworthiness. A brand name is usually legally registered as a trademark with a governmental organization to prevent other companies from using it. A brand is usually established in customer's minds through marketing, particularly advertising, and by satisfying customer experiences with the product or service. A brand is valuable to a company in encouraging repeat purchases and in extending the brand, with its aura of quality and trustworthiness, to new products and services. Examples of widely known and successful brands include Coca Cola (a trademark of the Coca Cola Company) and Amazon (a trademark of Amazon, Inc.). Branding (the establishment of a brand) is generally judged to be extremely important in electronic commerce because of the ease with which customers can find, compare, and do business with a wide variety of competitive companies offering similar products and service on the Internet.

brand marketing. Concept of marketing a product, service, or company to identify its distinctive benefits and qualities.

break even analysis. Break Even Analysis refers to the calculation to determine how much product a company must sell in order to break even on that product. It is an effective analysis to measure the impact of different marketing decisions. It can focus on the product, or incremental changes to the product to determine the potential outcomes of marketing tactics. The formula for a break even analysis is:

Break even point ($) = (Total Fixed Costs + Total Variable Costs).

Total Variable Costs = Variable cost per unit x units sold

Unit contribution (contribution margin) = Price per unit — Variable cost per unit.

When looking at making a change to the marketing program, one can calculate the incremental break even volume, to determine the merits of the change. This determines the required volume needed such that there is no effect to the company due to the change.

If making changes to fixed costs (changing advertising expenditure etc.):

Incremental break even volume = change in expenditure / unit contribution.

Thus if a company increased its advertising expenditure by $1 million, and its unit contribution for the specific product is $20, then the company would need to sell an additional 50,000 units to break even on the decision.

If making changes to the unit contribution (change in price, or variable costs):

Incremental break even volume = (Old Unit Volume x (Old Unit Contribution — New Unit Contribution)) / New Unit Contribution

Thus if a company increased its price from $15 to $20, and had variable costs of $10, it is increasing its unit contribution from $5 to $10, assume also an old unit volume of 1 million. It could therefore reduce its volume by 500,000 to break even on the decision.

When making changes to a specific product, cannibalization of other products may occur. To calculate the effect of cannibalization, the Break Even Cannibalization rate for a change in a product is:

New Product Unit Contribution / Old Product Unit Contribution.

New Product is the planned addition to a product line (or change to a product within a product line), Old Product is the product that loses sales to the new product (or the product line that loses sales). The cannibalization rate refers to the percentage of new product that would have gone to the old product, this must be lower than the break even cannibalization rate in order for the change to be profitable.

brick-and-mortar. A traditional business operation that commonly deals with its customers face-to-face in an office or store that the business owns or rents (e.g. a retail store or a bank branch). Web-based businesses usually have lower costs and greater flexibility than brick-and-mortar operations.

broadband. Broadband refers to the ability of the user to view content across the internet that includes large files, such as video, audio and 3D. Broadband refers to an increased ability to do so. The term narrowband can refer to the inability to do so. A user's broadband capability is typically governed by the last mile issue, the connection between the ISP and the user. Once broadband is no longer an issue, the web is likely to become much more useful!

Broadband Web. A vision of the future World Wide Web with high speed broadband connections to the home and desktop. The Broadband Web is expected to pose a significant threat to CD-ROM use and to favor high quality small independent multimedia developers who can afford to offer their products on the Web but who cannot afford to mass market a CD-ROM.

broker. An individual or company that is an intermediary between a seller and a buyer. A stockbroker specializes in stocks, bonds and other investments.

bugs: A bug is the term used to describe a coding error in a computer program. Bugs can be discovered throughout the development process. As systems are tested with live users (through alpha and beta versions), and systems become more interrelated, bugs tend to surface that were not recognized during the early stages of development.

(product) bundling. Product Bundling refers to the bundling together of more than one product for a sale. This is very common for digital products, where the marginal costs of each product is very low. If most of the marginal cost is associated with packaging and distribution, this is further reduced when the products are bundled together, as they share the same costs of packaging and distribution. Thus the incremental cost to the firm (i.e. Microsoft!) for bundling together additional software products is very small (actually zero aside from any opportunity cost). Thus a suite of products may allow for greater market penetration into different software markets than if the software was sold separately. For software that is not currently used by the consumer, but is purchased through a bundled package, it works to lock-in the consumer once he/she decides to use that category of software. Thus bundled software can ensure strong market positions across multiple markets.

While product bundling is a regular phenomena for software and related products, product unbundling may occur in the traditional content provider markets as microtransactions can provide payment options for smaller increments of the product. Thus rather than having to buy an entire CD (a bundling of different song titles, mostly of little relevance to each other) the consumer may be able to pay for a single song title, unbundled.

burn-rate. Burn-rate refers to the amount of money a company spends from month to month (money burnt) in order to survive. Thus a burn-rate of $50,000 would mean the company spends $50,000 a month above any incoming cash flow to sustain its business. Entrepreneurial companies will calculate their burn-rate in order to understand how much time they have before they need to raise more money, or show a positive cash flow.

button. A small advertisement that can provide a constant presence on a Web site while costing considerably less than a banner. Buttons can build brand awareness and attract traffic to the sponsor's Web site but their message must be limited and simple.

button ads. Similar to banner ads, except they are smaller than the standard 468 by 60 pixel banner ads. Standard dimensions include square button (125 x 125 pixels), button 1 (120 x 90), button 2 (120 x 60) and micro bar (88 x 31).

byte. Group of eight bits used to represent a character such as a letter (a), number (1), or typographic symbol (?).

cable connection. One of the fastest growing of available Internet connection types, particularly among cable television subscribers. Cable connections require cable modems to provide a relatively low cost, very high speed download, a reasonably fast upload rate, and an "always on" connection to the Internet.

cache. High speed memory that stores data for relatively short periods of time, under computer control, in order to speed data transmission or processing. Web pages that are used frequently are often cached close to users so that they can be delivered quickly without requiring repeated transmissions over the entire network between the Web server and the client machine.

cache busting. Preventing browsers or proxy servers from serving content from their cache, in order to force the browser or proxy server to fetch a fresh copy for each user request. Cache busting is used to provide a more accurate count of the number of requests from users.

Call Detail Reporting. (1)The logging and reporting of details about each connection by users to a LAN through a network access server. (2) The logging and reporting by a PBX of voice or data calls made from the PBX to the Public-Switched Telephone Network or vice-versa.

call to action. Call to Action is the action that is requested by a marketer's content (either from an advertising banner or web-site copy). This may be to click-through to enter a contest, enter a survey to win a free prize or purchase a product.

cannibalization. Cannibalization refers to the notion of a company making a conscious business decision that will have a negative impact on either a current product or member of a distribution channel (or entire channel, via disintermediation). This type of decision is typically designed to allow the company to survive in the long-term, and avoid having its products challenged by competitors' products as technology progresses.

canonical domain names (CNAME). Sub-sets (prefixes as it were) of your main domain name which point to the same place. For example, mail.yoursite.com and members.yoursite.com.

CAP. Competitive Access Provider. A company which competes with local telephone companies to provide access from the customer's premise to long distance carriers. Currently the largest CAP in the U.S. is Teleport Communications Group.

CAPI. Cryptography API.

captive market. A captive market is a group of consumers who have limited choice in terms of the products they can select/purchase (no choice)! This type of market was common during the production era when there was a limited supply of goods (and great demand). It occurs when the market is monopolistic, thus there is only one supplier in the marketplace. This is more likely to occur with digital products (Microsoft is a good example of this). It can occur when a marketer has achieved significant lock-in for its installed based. Thus the switching costs for the consumer to try a competing product become prohibitive.

card issuing bank. The bank that issued a credit or debit card (bankcard) to an individual or company.

card reader in the dispenser (CRIND). See automated fuel terminal.

cascading style sheets. Utilities that allow designers to apply many predefined page display styles to Web pages.

CC (Carbon Copy). Insert email addresses into the CC field of an outgoing email to send an email to one or more recipients.

CCITT V series. Several international modem standards set by the Consultative Committee for International Telephony and Telegraphy. The standards help buyers make sure modems they buy will communicate with other modems. The standards, formerly used primarily outside the United States, have been accepted almost universally since the advent of the 2400 bits per second (bps) modems. Not all are relevant to computer users. Examples include: V.21, V.22, V.22bis, V.23, V.26, V.26bis, V.27, V.27bis, V.27ter, V.29, V.32, V.32bis, V.34, V.42, V.42bis.

CDR. See Call Detail Reporting

Cello. A World Wide Web browser developed at Cornell University and integrated with gopher, WAIS, USENET and E-mail tools.

CERT (Computer Emergency Response Team). A clearinghouse of information about network security.

certification path. The hierarchy of certificate authorities that vouch for a digital certificate issued to a user. The path runs from the issuing certificate authority to the root certificate authority.

certification authority (CA). an agency that issues digital certificates to organizations or individuals.

certified delivery server. A server which uses public key cryptography to provide a destination non-repudiation service, similar to certified mail. The server establishes that a message was received or that a good faith effort was made to deliver it.

CFML (Cold Fusion Markup Language). An extension of HTML. A proprietary markup language used by Macromedia's ColdFusion MX to link HTML pages to database servers. CFML goes beyond database management to fill some important gaps in HTML, including session variables, branching logic, loops, and other constructs that programmers are accustomed to using, such as error trapping and debugging tools.

CGI (Common Gateway Interface). (1) A protocol that allows Web servers to interact dynamically with other software packages to create custom Web pages. (2) A Web server scripting standard; a mechanism used to connect script to Web servers. In the past, most CGI programs were actually script files and were often written in scripting languages like *PERL*. Today, scripts can also be executable programs. You can write scripts in C and *Visual Basic*. The CGI specification has gone through several revisions. The best place to fine up-to-date information is the *World Wide Web Consortium* (W3) Web site (http://www.w3.org).

CGI scripts. Commonly used to handle forms, database search queries on Web pages, and to produce dynamic Web page content. The CGI Resource Index is a popular directory offering thousands of CGI/Perl scripts.

channel. A Web page or category of information in a particular area of interest that is automatically delivered to a user's computer.

channel conflict. A set of problems posed by the offering of the same or similar products from the same manufacturer to the same customers through multiple distribution channels. Channel conflict tends to decrease prices and erode profit margins, particularly for intermediaries, and may lead to the refusal of intermediaries to continue selling the products.

channels. An Internet technology based upon server push which broadcasts information to Web browsers so that users can view the information passively, as with television, rather than interactively as in traditional Web use.

Channel Definition Format. A specification developed by Microsoft and PointCast that defines when and how Web browser users receive information broadcast over the Internet using server push technology.

chargebacks. Transactions debited to a merchant's account usually as a result of a cardholder dispute.

chat rooms. Places for Web users with a common interest to communicate in real-time.

check card. See off-line debit card.

check image interchange. The transmission of digitized images of checks between banks as part of the check clearing process. Since each check image requires approximately 40,000 bytes, images are not expected to replace paper checks soon. The first likely use will be as part of notification from one bank to another when the bank on which a large-dollar check is drawn decides not to honor the check and desires to provide the image of the check to the bank which originally accepted the check so that fraud or other problems can be rapidly investigated. Currently such notification is done by phone or Fed Wire. See presentment.

check-by-phone. A technology developed by Accelerated Payment Systems and EIS International to support the acceptance of checks by phone. Agents record checking account information, print and deposit facsimile checks, and send acknowledgments to all parties to a transaction.

CIX (Commercial Internet Exchange). A pact between network providers that allows them to do accounting for commercial traffic.

CLEC. See competitive local exchange carrier.

clearing. The process of managing the details between an acquirer and an issuer to allow posting of a cardholder's account and reconciliation of a merchant's settlement position.

click. On the Web, the act of selecting and following a link by placing one's mouse cursor on the text, graphics, banner, or button identifying the link and depressing a button on the mouse. See click-through rate.

click stream. The Web sites and Web pages a user visits, either in a single online session or over a longer period of time. Information about a user's click stream on a single site, and some information about the click stream over multiple sites, can be collected by specialized organizations using cookies. The information can be used to improve Web sites, customize Web sites, and to target appropriate marketing messages from ad-serving systems.

click-through count. The number of visitors who click on a Web advertisement link and go to the advertiser's Web site.

click-through rate. The percent of individuals viewing a Web page who click on a specific banner ad appearing on the page. Overall click-through rates have declined substantially since the early days of electronic commerce on the Web.

client. Any program you use to access a server; a computer application that requests support from another program (often called a *server*), which usually runs on a remote computer. For example, *Netscape Navigator* is a client that accesses programs (and Web pages) from servers on the Internet.

client errors. Errors that occur due to an invalid request by the visitor's browser. Client errors are in the 400-range. See return code.

clip art. Prepared artwork designed for use in Web pages by experts and novices alike.

cloaking. Also known as *stealth forwarding* or *URL forwarding*, this service lets you disguise a Web site that is hosted by a third-party web host provider to look like your own, with its own your-domain-specific URL. For example,

User enters: http://www.yourdomain.com/
User is forwarded to:
http://www.somefreehostprovider.com/users/yoursite/
URL in the address bar reads:
http://www.yourcomain.com/
User is none the wiser

closed loop reporting. The ability to measure the effectiveness of a particular ad on the Web by tracking which ad viewers actually bought which product, requested a catalog, or took other specific actions on the Web site.

clustering/clustered results. Clustering is a technique used by search engines to "cluster" search results together, when they find multiple results from the same Web site. Usually, the most relevant result is listed first with the other relevant pages from that same site indented below it.

This makes search results clearer and more useful to searchers, by preventing a small number of sites occupying all of the top rankings.

CMW+. The first commercial implementation, by Security First Network Bank, of the trusted operating system.

co-branding. Loosely, the appearance of two company names on a Web page or Web site, implying that a product or service is provided jointly by the two companies. Often the site belongs to a company with a significant customer base, market awareness or marketing power while the other company on the page or site is actually providing the bulk of the product or service. In another variety of co-branding, an advertiser provides information about its offering in the midst of ostensibly objective information on the site.

COCA. Cost of cracking adjustment. An adjustment in the strength of an encryption method over time to reflect that newer and faster computers are able to crack codes more rapidly. The adjustment is generally expressed as the bits that should be added to a key each year to maintain the cost of cracking the code at a constant level.

code. 1.A cipher. A mathematical function for encryption and decryption. 2. A software program or part of a software program.

colocated hosting. Self-hosting wherein the server is owned by the online store but is located at the Web host's site. The Web host provides maintenance based on the level of service the online business requires.

colocation/co-location/collocation. The provision of space for a customer's own computer server in the the Internet service provider's premises.

comment tags. Used by Web designers to add comments (<!—

comment —>) to a Web page and also to hide JavaScript code from non-compliant Web browsers.

commerce service provider (CSP). A Web host that also provides commerce hosting services on their computer.

commoditization. An increase in the number, availability, and similarity of products in a given category which tends to drive down the price of the products. Some people believe the rapid and easy access to information about products on the Internet will make markets more efficient, facilitate comparisons, increase competition, eliminate inconsequential differences between products, and drive toward commoditization and lower prices. Others believe that low marketing and distribution costs will enable companies to differentiate their products and establish a wide variety of niche markets.

communications software. Also referred to as telecommunications software, this software allows one computer to connect with other computers across telephone lines (via modems) and share information. Communications software transmits instructions to your modem that directs it to make connections, transfer files, and carry out other procedures.

community. In the context of the Internet and electronic commerce, people who participate in a online discussion group or bulletin board, or who return frequently to a Web site because of a common interest in a given subject. One business strategy developing on the Internet is to create a community and then sell access to the group for marketing purposes.

competitive local exchange carrier (CLEC). A company that competes with the established local telephone company to provide at least voice connections to the Public Switched Telephone Network (PSTN) to residences and business in the area served. CLECs are becoming integrated communications providers (ICPs) by adding data and other services. Also see incumbent local exchange carrier.

COM port (Communications Port). A plug-in socket in back of the computer for hooking up devices such as modems.

computationally secure. A cipher is computationally secure if systematic analysis with available computing resources cannot break the cipher in a short enough time to allow exploitation.

computer forensics. The field responsible for the collection, preservation, and analysis of computer-related evidence.

connect time. The period during which a user is signed on, usually for a fee, to an online service, bulletin board system, host computer, or Internet service provider.

Consumer Internet Privacy Protection Act of 1997. A law that regulates how interactive computer services can use personal information input by users. For the purposes of this bill, interactive computer services are essentially Internet service providers. See data protection.

contact card. A smart card in which the microchip is visible and makes contact with a reader to support digital cash or access control.

contactless card. A smart card which hides the microchip within the plastic and communicates through radio waves. Toll collection, where drivers hold their cards up to a reader as they pass, is the most common application. Contactless cards have been developed by AT&T Smart Cards and GemPlus Card International.

container. See tag and element.

content centric software. As distinguished from older processing-centric software in which content (data) is fed to the program, content centric software is embedded in or wrapped around content. It is oriented to dynamic documents and is generally designed to run over networks, including the World Wide Web.

Content Management System (CMS). System used to manage the content of a Web site. Typically, a CMS consists of two elements; the content management application (CMA) and the content delivery application (CDA).

conversion rate. The percentage of people who take a desired action (click, register, subscribe, buy, etc.).

contextual marketing. Contextual marketing is marketing that occurs in the context of when a person is more likely to be interested in the product/industry. Thus, a page sponsorship can be considered contextual, as the viewer has elected to view the page, and assuming the sponsorship is for a product that is related to the content of the page, the product has the right context (the viewer self-selected to view the content). Text advertisements that are relevant to the content of the web page they appear are another example of contextual marketing. An example of this is the advertising programs run by search engines that have advertisements dependent on the keywords being searched upon.

Contextual Marketing will also become more evident with the evolution of wireless marketing (m-commerce). Wireless marketing will take advantage of knowing where the consumer is located using GPS. This can then translate into marketing messages that have direct relevance to the consumer as the messages relate to the context of the consumer at the point in time they are being delivered.

Contribution Margins (Margins). Contribution margins (or margins) refer to the amount of revenue per product that is available to "contribute" towards the fixed costs and the profit of the company. Since, for digital products, the variable costs are typically very small, or zero, most of the revenue earned from the sale of a product form the contribution margin. Assuming the contribution margin (unit price - unit variable cost) > 0, then the product is worth marketing, since the fixed costs are sunk. This also assumes the product does not cannibalize sales from another product in the product line, if so, the opportunity costs need to be considered.

cookie, cookies. (1) Small bits of data that a Web server stores on a user's computer. Cookies have become a valuable way to keep track of a visitor's movements on your site, as sell as a convenient method to customize content based on a visitor's past preferences. A Cookie, for instance, allows a Web site to "recognize" and "remember" individual visitors by storing files on their browsers with a record of the last visit. Cookies cannot be used to "see" any other data on the user's computer, nor can they determine the user's e-mail address or identity. (2) Files containing information about visitors to a Web site. This information can include the visitor's username, preferences, and other information. The information is collected by the Web server and delivered to the visitor's computer during their first visit to a Web site. The server records the information in a text file and stores it on the visitor's hard drive. At the beginning of each subsequent visit, the server reads this information and configures itself based on the information provided.

cookie blocker. A third-party program the prevents cookie storage selectively.

cookie buster. Software that blocks cookies from being placed on a user's browser.

Cookie File. The cookie file is a file that resides on the client machine. It contains data passed from web sites, so that web sites can communicate with this file when the same client returns. The web site only has access to the part of the cookie file that represents the interaction with that particular web site. Clearly the cookie file has caused some issues with respect to privacy. Considering that as consumers, we do not know what information is being stored in the file, we should become concerned! The cookie file was first developed in order to help sites with the transaction process of the web. Without a cookie file, web sites are not able to track a single user's path through a web site, thus a transaction that required multiple pages (as most do) would simply not be workable.

CoSN (Consortium of School Networks). A nonprofit group whose members include K-12 teachers, hardware and software vendors, and Internet Service Providers (ISPs).

cost-per-click (CPC). A method of charging for banner advertisements on the Web on the basis of how many viewers click on the ad, rather than charging on a flat rate basis for the advertising space. The CPC model is generally considered to favor advertisers rather than publishers because it ignores the brand building value of an ad that is seen but not clicked on, generally gives the publisher no control over the content or appearance of the ad, and may require the publisher to allocate space to poorly performing ads until the contracted number of clicks have been achieved.

cost-per-thousand (CPM). The cost in any given media for a thousand impressions. On the Web, the CPM for impressions on a Web site that attracts an undifferentiated variety of consumers (e.g. a typical search engine) is on the order of $5. The CPM for advertising on a Web site with a very specific audience that is likely to make sizable purchases (e.g. corporate telecommunications managers) can be in the neighborhood of $100. See targeting.

countermeasure. A physical or logical procedure that recognizes, reduces, or eliminates a threat.

country club billing. A system in which each charge slip is returned to the credit card customer along with the customer's bill. Until 1976, credit card companies were required to provide costly country club billing. See descriptive billing.

CPM, CPC, CPA. CPM (Cost per 1,000), CPC (Cost per Click) and CPA (Cost per Action) are methods of calculating the charge for pages (advertisements) being served. CPM is a holdover from traditional media advertising, and does not take advantage of the Hypertext nature of the medium. It charges purely on the number of times the advertisement is served. It does account for branding effects, that are not accounted for in the other models. CPC is a cost associated with each click on the advertisement to the target page. CPA is a cost associated with each lead created from a click on the advertisement (CPL), or each sale (CPS). Both CPC and CPA are much more accountable means of developing a price for the banner, and either are also used for affiliate programs. They become a variable cost in terms of generating the number of people exposed to the target page (this number is based on the CTR from the host vehicle), the number of leads generated (CPL) or the number of sales (CPS). The downside for the vehicles is they do not control the design of the banner (poor design = low click-through etc.) and they are not rewarded for the branding effect of the banner.

CPL (Cost-Per-Lead). Cost to an advertiser for each lead generated by an affiliate.

CPO (Cost-Per-Order). Cost of advertising based on the number of orders received.

CPS (Cost-Per-Sale). Cost, in terms of a commission payment, to an advertiser for each sale generated by an affiliate.

CPT (Cost-Per-Transaction). Cost of advertising based on the number of transactions received.

cracker. Someone who attempts to thwart computer security systems.

crawlers/spiders/bots. Programs that visit and read Web pages in order to create entries for a search engine index.

creatives. Banner ads, copy, active URLs and other forms of creative artwork which are due to the ad seller prior to the initiation of an ad campaign.

CRC (Cyclic Redundancy Check). An error-checking procedure for data transmission. The sending device performs a complex calculation, generating a number based upon the data being transmitted, and sends that number to the receiving device. The receiving device performs the same calculation after transmission. If the results match, the transmission succeeds. If the numbers don't match, it means the message was received in an altered state, and the data may be incorrect.

credit transfer. A transfer of funds in which the payer issues a payment order to the payer's own bank and the order is passed, possibly through intermediary banks, to the bank of the payee or beneficiary. (See debit transfer.)

CRM. CRM (Customer Relationship Management) is a business strategy built around the concept of being customer-centric. The main goals are to optimise revenue through improved customer satisfaction via improved interactions at each customer touch point. This can be accomplished by a better understanding of customers, based on their purchasing patterns and demographics, and better information empowerment at all customer touch points, whether with employees or other media interfaces.

CRON script. A list of one or more commands to a computer operating system or application server that are to be executed (processed) at a specified time.

cryptography API. An application program interface that makes it easy for applications to use cryptography software developed by others. It facilitates application development, supports updating of the application code and the cryptography code independent of one another, and allows the use of different cryptography code for domestic sales (in the USA) and for export. (See export laws.)

Cryptoki. A standard application program interface that presents applications with a simple object view of a device called a cryptographic token. The logical token definition is independent of the underlying cryptographic technology. The Cryptoki Standard (also known as PKCS #11) was developed by RSA Data Security. See crypto API.

Cryptolopes. The specific implementation of secure containers implemented in IBM's infoMarket.

C shell. A user interface for those whose Internet providers offer only character-based, command-line access to a Unix system (hence the term "shell account").

CSS (Cascading Style Sheets). CSS defines how to display HTML elements in a Web page.

CTI. Computer Telephony Integration.

CTR. CTR (Click-Through Rate) is the number of times an advertisement is clicked upon over the number of times the advertisement is served. Typical click-through rates have been declining (a click through rate of 1% would be very high). The click-through rate will determine the cost of an advertising campaign that was based on CPC and CPA.

customer acquisition cost. The cost of acquiring a new customer.

cybercafes. Establishments, usually coffee shops, which offer Internet access to the public.

cybermediary. An individual or organization that collects a fee for facilitating transactions over the Internet without taking ownership of the products or services sold. Also see Internet Transaction Broker. Examples include Web sites that provide many of the services of traditional real estate brokers and insurance agents but at much lower costs.

cybersquatting. The practice of registering a domain name that is the trademark of another person or company with the hope that the trademark owner will pay huge amounts of money for the rights to the domain.

cyber vandalism. The electronic defacing of an existing Web page.

CyberWallet. A technology for enabling secure transactions over networks developed by V-ONE Corporation and designed to run in conjunction with World Wide Web browsers. It will hold information on up to 16 credit cards or bank accounts. It is especially designed to prevent merchant fraud and is based on Secure Transaction Channel technology (see STC). CyberWallet has been licensed to Checkfree and Spyglass as part of the Electronic Business Co-op (EBC).

cycling. Replacing the oldest log file with the newest log file.

databases. Collection of data that is organized so that its contents can be easily accessed, managed, and updated.

datagram. A formatted set of electronic data used in communication between computer systems. Datagrams consist of two parts: the *data proper* (which may be part of a longer message), and the *header* (which indicates the *source*, the *destination*, and the *type* of data).

data mining. Looking for hidden patterns in data.

data protection. The prevention of the passing of an individual's personal information from one computer system where the information legitimately resides to other computer systems without the consent of the individual. In the United Kingdom the Data Protection Act of 1984 requires the registration of every data user who processes personal information.

DAVIC (Digital Audio Video Interactive Council). A committee which sets standards for digital transmission of multimedia in Europe. See DOCSIS.

DDN (Defense Data Network). A segment of the Internet that links to US military bases and contractors around the world. Used for unsecured communications.

dead link. A Web link that, when clicked, displays an error message instead of a Web page. See return code.

debit transfer. A transfer of funds in which the payer issues a payment order to the payee, the payee takes the order to the payee's bank and the order is passed back to the payer's bank in exchange for the actual funds. Consumer payments by check are a type of debit transfer. (See credit transfer.)

DECnet. A set of proprietary networking protocols utilized (instead of TCP/IP) by Digital Equipment Corporation's operating systems. These protocols are not compatible with the Internet.

decryption. Process of interpreting data which is sent in a hard to read form (encrypted).

dedicated servers. Computers that include a Web server, related software, and connection to the Internet, housed in a Web hosting company's premises, that can be rented exclusively for your own use.

deep linking. Linking to a page other than the site's home page.

de-listing. Removal of pages from a search engine's index.

demilitarized zone (DMZ). An area of an organization's network which is open to the public over the Internet and is separated from the organization's private network by a firewall. The resources in the demilitarized zone are typically Web servers and are often outsourced by the organization to an Internet Service Provider which locates the DMZ at the ISP's point of presence (POP).

Demographics. In marketing, the description of a group of consumers, most often age, gender, household income, level of education, marital status, employment status, number of people in the household, and region of the country. More loosely, a description of any group of customers whether consumers or businesses. See targeting.

DES (Data Encryption Standard). An encryption standard adopted by the US government for encrypting sensitive information.

description tag. HTML meta tag used to provide a description of a Web page for search engine listings.

descriptive billing. A system of credit card billing in which individual charge slips are not returned with the bill. Federal Reserve Board Regulation Z requires that if a charge slip is not enclosed, the bill must provide the date, the amount, the seller's name and the location where the transaction took place for each transaction.

DHCP (Dynamic Host Configuration Protocol). A communications protocol that gives network administrators a central place to manage and automate the assignment of Internet Protocol (IP) addresses in an organization's network.

DHTML (dynamic HTML). Advanced version of HTML that contains more features, for example, animation.

dial-up. (Compare leased line). A telecommunications medium that links computers using regular telephone lines, generally referring to the kind of connection one makes when using a terminal emulator and a regular modem.

dial-up connection. A method of connecting to an Internet service provider using a telephone connection in a system of many lines shared by many users. A dial-up connection can be started manually or automatically by a computer's modem or other device.

differential work factor cryptography. A technology embedded in Lotus Notes Release 4.0 that allows export of 64 bit cryptography without special permits (see export law) while assuring the US government that government agencies can decrypt messages encoded using the technology as easily as they can decrypt conventional 40 bit cryptography. The government generated a public/private key pair and gave the public key to Lotus. Lotus uses this public key to bind into each Lotus Notes 64 bit key a 24 bit work factor reduction capability. A cracker must still decrypt a 64 key.

Diffie-Hellman. A public key algorithm which can be used for deriving and distributing private keys over insecure networks. Diffie-Hellman itself cannot be used to encrypt or decrypt messages. The patent on the algorithm expired on April 29, 1997.

(technology) diffusion process. The diffusion process refers to the process of adoption of new products by the consumer marketplace. The consumer marketplace is segmented into four groups: innovators (2.5% of population), early adapters (13.5%), early majority (34%), late majority (34%), and laggards (16%). Thus innovators are more likely to adopt a new product earlier than the early majority etc. This has implications for target marketing with new products.

digital certificate/signature. Electronic "credit card" that establishes your credentials when doing business or other transactions on the Web.

digital products. Digital products are intangible products that can be transferred over a digital network. They have zero copy costs, and users can make perfect copies. The cost structure of digital products (high fixed costs that are sunk, and tending towards zero marginal costs) in conjunction with the above features changes the economics of digital products vs. traditional goods.

Digital Subscriber Line (DSL). A technology that allows the transmission of many forms of data, voice, and video for limited distances over the standard twisted-pair copper wire that is widely used to connect home and business telephone lines to telephone company central offices. DSL generally offers much higher transmission speeds than standard modems or ISDN but lower speeds (i.e. less bandwidth) than cable modems or T1 lines.

digital videodisk technology. See DVD.

diminishing returns. Diminishing returns refers to the notion that the return that a company receives for additional effort decreases as the number of units/ output increases. This is typical of industrial goods, but is in contrast to the phenomena of network effects and increasing returns for digital goods. Diminishing returns explains why industrial companies become more ineffecient once they grow over a certain size. Thus firms do not compete as effectively when in a *large* monopolistic market than they do in an oligopolistic market (car company for example) assuming the size of the market is over the scale limit that traditional firms can operate efficiently. With the "winner takes all" behavior of digital goods, markets can be more efficient when one company supplies the entire marketplace, especially if the market is governed by proprietary standards versus open standards.

DirecPC. A service from Hughes Network Systems that uses a VSAT antenna and a PC card to capture satellite broadcasts and download large files at 1.5 to 2 Mbits per second. Requests for files are sent by users using modems over telephone lines.

Direct Hit. This search engine used to provide search results by analyzing the activity of millions of previous Internet searchers. Since Teoma, another popular search engine, acquired the technology behind Direct Hit, the search interface is no longer publicly accessible.

directory. A structure for organizing files on a computer or on a network. Directories may be protected or shared using various methods for information security. Common directory structures include NetWare Directory Services, X.500 (a standard), and Banyan Vines.

directory service. A service on a network that relays information about sites, computers, resources, or users in the area.

directory service markup language (DSML). A language which allows XML enabled applications, particularly electronic commerce applications, to share information from a variety of directories without knowing the specific data formats for each vendor's directory. The language extends the LDAP (lightweight directory access protocol) to Web applications.

discussion boards and chat rooms. Discussion boards allow for asynchronous discussion between 2 or more people over a period of time. Chat rooms are designed for synchronous discussion at one time. Discussion boards are typically available for review, at any time, chat rooms have no data until a chat session begins.

Discussion boards are useful to allow many people to become involved in online "conversations" over a period of time. A site that has used discussion boards effectively is slashdot.org. This site is a community that serves as a meeting place for those interested in the advancement of all things digital, as they say: "News for nerds!" The site's content essentially is created by its community, which in turn becomes more closely associated with the site as they are developing the site. Other sites attempt to achieve this without as much success. Slashdot's success lies in its structure: initial discussion content short, but with enough information to establish context, this allows discussion to follow. The ClueTrain Manifesto, while being radical in its approach and view points, makes a compelling case for commercial sites to include a discussion board to allow for conversations among consumers, and between consumers and employees. The Student 2 student aspect of the Wharton MBA Admissions site follows this advise. The content on this site is content marketing could not pay for, and comes from credible sources.

Chat Rooms are useful for gathering people together for "quick" events that are centered around specific topics. They are very good for brainstorming events, and to resolve problems that need quick discussion. Chat rooms are often used in conjunction with discussion boards to satisfy communication needs of the organization. Unfortuntely the terms, discussion boards and chat rooms, are often confused, people refering the two as chat rooms. Instant Messenging is another form of communication evolving on the internet.

discussion forums. Web sites where people meet for open discussion on various topics.

disintermediation. Disintermediation refers to the potential for members of traditional value chains (distribution channels) to become obsolete as the producer markets more directly with its consumers using the web. This occurs with legacy businesses. While channels (using the web) are presumed to become shorter, in reality, the channels actually include different types of intermediaries (infomediaries) such as meta-markets (also referred to as industry portals) that help gather many industry players and consumers into a market*space*.

disruptive technology. This is a technology that changes the industry in such a way that previous competitive and business rules do not apply. Since the internet has had such a profound effect on the fundamental rules of business, it can be considered a disruptive technology. CD technology was another good example of a disruptive technology. When CDs were introduced to the music business, they were a disruptive technology, changing the status quo, and requiring users to purchase new hardware, despite there being a significant installed-base of record players and record collections.

distribution channel. A method by which a manufacturer or software developer delivers its goods to customers and receives payment in return. A direct channel, whereby the company transacts business with its customers with no intermediaries, is common in business-to-business commerce and in catalog sales, direct mail, or telemarketing to consumers. Indirect channels may use any variety of distributors, resellers, retailers, agents, or other intermediaries. In many indirect channels the goods are marketed using the brand of the manufacturer while sales, installation, service, and customer support are provided by an intermediary. In the original equipment manufacture (OEM) channel the product often takes on a brand owned by the intermediary and often becomes part of a more comprehensive offering by the intermediary. By making it easy for customers to find and do business with manufacturers, electronic commerce often makes a direct channel more cost effective for the manufacturer than it had previously been. See channel conflict.

DMZ. See demilitarized zone.

DNS (Domain Name Server). Machine which translates Internet domain names, such as www.google.com to IP (Internet Protocol) addresses such as 216.239.51.100 (one of Google's IP address).

DOCSIS (Data Over Cable Interface Specification). Cable modem specifications set by the MCNS group of cable operators in North America. See DAVIC.

document-type definition (DTD). See Extensible Markup Language.

DOD (Department of Defense). The branch of government whose *Advanced Research Projects Agency* (ARPAnet) began the creation of the Internet.

Dogpile. A metasearch engine that searches four search engines at a time and lists the results from each engine on each page.

DOM (Document Object Model). A platform and language-neutral interface that allows programs and scripts to dynamically access and update the content, structure, and style of documents.

domain. Name with which domain name server records are associated that describe subdomains or hosts.

domain name. A domain name (also known as host name) is an alphanumeric name that identifies a computer on the internet. While it is possible to reach computers on the internet by using the IP address, IP addresses are generally not easy to remember. Domain names provide an easily referenced way of reaching remote computers. The domain name is the first part of the web address or URL. For example, this web page's domain name is www.udel.edu

The Domain Name Service (DNS) stores a database of mappings from domain names to IP addresses and performs lookups for the IP address when a domain name is used in a network request. To avoid network congestion, lookups are performed on root servers with current copies of the central directory. These root servers are further copied by ISPs. To register a domain name for the .com, .org, .biz, .net, .info and .name, you can use one of the accredited registrars, and their resellers. ICANN.org is the accrediting agency that approves resellers and resolves disputes. You can learn about information behind the ownership of a domain name by using the WHOIS service. ccTLDs (country code top level domains, such as .uk, .at and .fr) are handled independently and visiting country's site is important to understand the rules.

domain name lookup. The process of converting a numeric IP address into a text name (for example, 206.113.230.3 converts to www.whaddup.com. You can see the reverse of this in action by typing ***ping www.whaddup.com*** (or any other domain name) at the command line. That will return the IP address of the domain name you specify. See ping.

Domain Name System (DNS). The unique name of a collection of computers connected to networks such as the Internet. A general-purpose, replicated, distributed data query service for looking up host IP addresses based on host names. The DNS is hierarchical, consisting of domains, subdomains, sites, and hosts. Unique names are formed from smallest to largest, and are of the form *user@host.site.subdomain.domain*, where *host* and *site* are often optional. On the Internet, domain names typically end with a suffix denoting the type of site:

- **.com** (commercial)
- **.edu** (educational)
- **.net** (network operations)
- **.gov** (US government)
- **.mil** (US military)
- **.org** (organization)
- **.us** (United States)
- **.ca** (Canada)
- **.uk** (United Kingdom)
- **.au** (Australia)
- **.cz** (Czech Republic)
- **.xx** (where ***xx*** refers to another country's two-letter abbreviation)

doorway/bridge/entry/gateway/information pages. Information pages created for the sole purpose of ranking high in search engines for a particular keyword phrase, or specific search engine.

dotted quad. The representation of an IP address; it appears as up to four separate numbers delineated by periods (for example 126.204.89.56).

download. Copying a file from a remote computer down to your local computer.

downstream. The connection that occurs when information is sent to a user's computer from an ISP.

DSL (Digital Subscriber Line). DSL is a technology that transmits high-bandwidth information over ordinary copper telephone lines. Individual connections will typically provide 512 Kbps to 1.544 Mbps downstream and 128 Kbps upstream transfer rates. A DSL line can carry both data and voice signals and the data part of the line is continuously connected.

DSML. See directory service markup language.

DTD. See Extensible Markup Language.

duality. The issuance of credit cards from both major bank card associations (Visa and MasterCard) by an individual bank.

dumb terminal. A terminal that doesn't contain an internal microprocessor. It responds to simple control codes, and usually displays only characters and numerals.

dutch auction. A type of open auction in which bidding starts at a high price and drops until a bidder accepts the price.

DVD. A technology that uses five inch discs similar to CD-ROMs but which can hold much more data. A DVD disc can deliver multi-channel sound and TV images three times sharper than videotape. DVD players, expected to debut in late 1996, will be interoperable with televisions, stereos, personal computers and some video games. Unlike CDs, DVDs can hold data on both sides and can provide either one or two layers of data on each side. A single-sided single layer DVD holds 4.7 gigabytes of data while a double-sided double-layer DVD holds 17 gigabytes.

dynamic ad rotation. Delivery of ads on a rotating, random basis so that visitors are exposed to different ads in different pages of a site.

dynamically generated pages. Database driven Web pages created "on the fly," depending on the user's interest or request.

dynamic content. Non-static information constructed in response to a Web client's request

dynamic HTML (DHTML). Instructions written in HTML that enable Web pages to react to user input and produce content that changes each time it is viewed. With dynamic HTML coding, Web pages are created "on the fly", as the information is delivered to your desktop. There are many technologies for producing dynamic HTML, including CGI scripts, Server-Side Includes (SSI), cookies, *Java, JavaScript, Cold Fusion* and *ActiveX.*

dynamic page. A Web page whose content is shaped by a program in response to a user request. Web page that respond to users' requests and gather information from them. Oftentimes, they have built-in links to a relational database, from which they extract data based on input from the user (using dynamic SQL). Dynamic Web pages contain very little actual text. Instead, they pull needed information from other applications. Dynamic Web pages communicate with databases to extract employee directory information, spreadsheets to display accounting figures, client-server database management systems to interact with order processing applications, and more.

dynamic pricing. Dynamic Pricing refers to a fluid pricing scheme between the buyer and seller, rather than the more traditional (and more recent, over the last 100 years) fixed pricing. Dynamic pricing is a legacy from the past, that has losts its significance with the advent of the industrial revolution and mass marketing and mass communication. Before the industrial revolution, most trade occured in markets, with many buyers and sellers bartering for goods.

Current, and evolving models for dynamic pricing include the auction pricing system, group pricing system and reverse pricing system. Typically these systems will better reflect the true market value of the product involved, but also require additional work on the part of the purchaser. These systems will evolve more rapidly when better standards are established and when intelligent agents evolve. Not all markets will be served well with a dynamic pricing model.

dynamic SQL. This feature modifies queries based on user data, environment variables, and previously returned query results. Dynamic SQL can also increase processing efficiency by executing multiple queries and sending them to multiple databases from a single browser request.

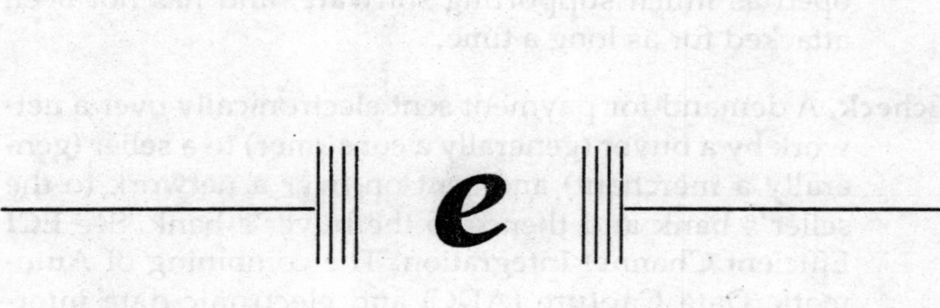

EARN (European Academic and Research Network). The European equivalent to BITNET.

EADP. Emergency Access Demonstration Program A federal program to demonstrate the feasibility of using key recovery in federal business applications.

EAI. See Enterprise Application Integration.

e-books/ebooks. Electronic books that can be read on a personal computer or a special e-book reader.

e-Business (e-Mail, e-Commerce, e-Zine, e-Solution, e-Market, e-Service, etc.). Oftentimes used without the hyphen, the «e» originally stood for «electronic», as in «online». Today the term is used rather freely to describe any situation or solution that has made the migration from real world to the Internet.

ECC. elliptic curve cryptosystem. An alternative to the RSA encryption system which is based on the difficulty of solving elliptic curve discrete logarithm problems rather than on factoring large numbers. Developed and marketed by Certicom, ECC is especially suitable for environments, such as wireless devices and PC cards, where computational power is limited and high speed is required. For any given key size (measured in bits) ECC provides more security (is harder to decrypt without the key) than RSA. ECC is newer than RSA, has not developed as much supporting software, and has not been attacked for as long a time.

Echeck. A demand for payment sent electronically over a network by a buyer (generally a consumer) to a seller (generally a merchant) and sent on over a network to the seller's bank and thence to the buyer's bank. See **ECI** Efficient Channel Integration. The combining of Automatic Data Capture (ADC) and electronic data interchange (EDI) to improve the timeliness and accuracy of production and delivery.

***E*Codestream.** Web Application Development and Integration services provider, based in Los Angeles, CA, and founded by Marcus W. Tremble. *E*Codestream develops, implements and manages three-tier, enterprise-level Web solutions. Slogans: "Web Solutions for the Conscious Enterprise" and "If their solutions aren't getting you there, they're not solutions".

E-commerce. E-commerce refers to all forms of business activities conducted across the internet. This can include E-tailing, B2B, intranets and extranets, online advertising (eg. advertising banners), and simply online presences of any form that are used for some type of communication (customer service for example).

economic profit. Return on investment in excess of the average cost of capital in the overall market. Alternatively, profits excluding profits from the increase in value of inventory which the company holds.

economies of scale. Economies of scale refers to the notion of increasing efficiencies of the production of goods as the number of goods being produced increases. Typically the average costs of producing a good will diminish as each additional good is produced, since the fixed costs are shared over an increasing number of goods.

Due to economies of scale, larger companies have greater access to markets in terms of selecting media to access those markets, and can operate with larger geographic reach.

For traditional companies, size does have its limits, where additional size actually increases costs to companies (impacts communications costs etc., diminishing returns). Thus many industries tend to operate more effectively in an oligopolistic fashion, with few large firms, rather than one monopolist. (This should occur even if the government allowed monopolists and monopolists behaved legally). Digital companies tend not to suffer from this size limitation.

ecosystem. An ecosystem is a system whose members benefit from each other's participation via symbiotic relationships (positive sum relationships). It is a term that originated from biology, and refers to self-sustaining systems.

The bumblebee hive is an example of an ecosystem, highlighted in Bernd Heinrich's book, Bumblebee Economics. The bumblebees' hive is a living system with one goal, to gather enough energy to ensure the survival of the bumblebee's genetic information. Bumblebees (unlike most other species) live in colonies and depend on each other for survival. Bumblebees extract pollen for protein and nectar for their sole source of energy from neighboring plants. Plants, in turn, rely on bumblebees to inadvertently brush pollen from one plant to another, to enable the plants' reproduction process to begin. The relationship between the bumblebee and the plant is symbiotic, as each benefits from each other's participation. The bumblebee hive goes through a life cycle, through the year. Entering the fall the queen bee lays eggs that are fed a different diet. These eggs turn into virgin queens and males. When the frost hits, the remaining worker bees die as does the queen, the virgin queens and males fly off, mate, the males die and the inseminated queens seek shelter through the winter. The process then begins again.

As it applies to business, an ecosystem can be viewed as a system where the relationships established across different industries become mutually beneficial, self-sustaining and (somewhat) closed. This is clearly the case for Silicon Valley with the entrepreneurial industry, the venture capital industry needed to fund the entrepreneurial industry, and Stanford University, supplying the human capital needed to develop innovative/creative ideas and technologies. The goal of this ecosystem is to generate entrepreneurial ventures. Once an ecosystem is established, and is able to take first-mover advantage, it becomes very difficult for other regions to emulate. The region exhibits network effects and is able to establish lock-in since the switching costs associated with moving to another region are prohibitive. The collective costs of many moving out of the region (i.e. if another region tried to incentivize a large move) would be prohibitive. Thus current members have a clear incentive to remain, and new would-be entrepreneurs, venture capitalists and students interested in this industry have a significant incentive to relocate to this region.

ECR. Electronic cash register

Edgar. Electronic Data Gathering, Analysis, and Retrieval System. A database available over the Internet that gives investors free and easy access to disclosure documents that publicly traded companies must file with the Securities and Exchange Commission (S.E.C).

EDI (Electronic Data Interchange). Exchange between businesses of computer-readable data in a standard format.

Edibanx EDI Bank Alliance Network. A payment system operated by the Chicago Clearing House Association for the paperless exchange of payments between companies using electronic data interchange (EDI) standard formats. Edibanx was developed by thirteen major banks in October, 1994, and recruited several other banks in the following year.

EFF (Electronic Frontier Foundation). A nonprofit organization concerned with Internet-related privacy and access issues.

EFT-POS (Electronic Funds Transfer at the Point-of-Sale). The automatic transfer of funds, using a debit card at a retail point of sale, from a consumer's demand deposit account to the retailer's account. EFT-POS transactions pass through the retailer's back office computer and, if the retailer is part of a chain, may also pass through the data center of the retailer on its way to the EFT processor.

electronic cash. A form of electronic payment which is anonymous and can be spent only once.

electronic bill delivery. A system from Visa Interactive which enables banks to electronically deliver bills to consumers through the consumer's PC or telephones. Eventually the system will allow consumers to send electronic payments back through their banks to the biller's accounts receivable system.

Electronic Check system. A project by the FSTC that allows customers to write and sign secure checks for transactions over insecure public networks, such as the Internet. The system uses crytographic processing in a PCMCIA card from Telequip Corporation to assure that the checks cannot be counterfeited or forged.

electronic rights. Copyrights extended to electronic media.

Electronic Signature Capture Terminals. From AT&T Global Information Systems, terminals that translate signatures into digital images and send them to a payment processing firm for storage.

electronic tax filing. A offering of the Internal Revenue Service that allows taxpayers to file their tax returns on diskette or over a network. In 1994, 11.8 million tax returns were filed electronically or about 11% of all individual tax returns. The number was down 15.8% from 1993 because of increased IRS efforts to prevent the fraud which can be facilitated when tax returns are filed electronically. Fraud has caused the IRS to question its goal of getting 80% of Americans to file electronically by the year 2001. See RAL.

electronic wallet. A software utility that holds electronic cash, credit card information, owner identification, and provides these data automatically at electronic commerce sites. There are two types: a client-side electronic wallet stores a consumer's information on the consumer's own computer and a server-side electronic wallet stores that information on a remote server that belongs to a particular merchant or to the wallet's publisher.

element. The basic building block of an HTML document. When an element consists of a start tag, an end tag, and text or some other content it can also be referred to as a "container". An "empty element", such as that commanding a line break, has only one tag and no content.

e-mail/electronic mail. Online communications between computer users. The most frequently used communications tool on the Internet. E-mail allows you to communicate with one or thousands of users in less time and for less money than it takes to communicate with another person via traditional phone or mail services.

email discussion lists. Similar to discussion forums, except the discussions are conducted via email, instead of on the Web.

email marketing. Marketing via electronic mail.

Encapsulating Security Payload (ESP). A fundamental element of IPsec that provides integrity, authentication, and confidentiality for IP datagrams. ESP works between hosts, between a host and a security gateway, or between security gateways. The support for security gateways (in Tunnel-mode) permits trustworthy networks behind a security gateway to omit encryption while using security gateways to obtain confidentiality for transmissions over untrustworthy network segments. In Tunnel-mode ESP encapsulates the entire IP datagram within the ESP. (See tunneling.) When there is no intervening security gateway, then the hosts may use the Transport-mode in which only the upper layer protocol data (e.g., TCP or UDP) is encrypted and there is no encrypted IP header. In Transport-mode ESP encapsulates an upper-layer protocol (e.g. UDP or TCP) inside ESP and then adds a cleartext IP header. This cleartext IP header is used to carry the protected data through the intervening networks. Transport-mode can reduce both the bandwidth consumed and the protocol processing costs for users that do not need to keep the entire IP datagram confidential or who encrypt the data in the host application prior to transmission. ESP works with both unicast and multicast traffic.

encryption. Process of encoding data into a form which is hard to read and decipher. This data can then be decoded (decrypted) by someone with the correct key.

encryption engine. A device planned by Hewlett-Packard and Gemplus SCA that would support basic encryption capabilities in a computer when combined with a separately installable policy card that controls the strength of the encryption algorithm. The combination permits the volume production and export from the US, without State Department approval, of computers potentially able to support many levels of encryption while still allowing State Department control of encryption strength (by approval or denial of the policy card) on an individual customer basis.

Enterprise Application Integration (EAI). The linking and sharing of multiple business applications and data, including extensions to business partners, through the use of application-to-application modules, object middleware and message brokering, or multitier application server platforms. Motivations for EAI include the need to rapidly implement Web-based projects, the need to link to legacy data, and the need to forge links to different systems acquired through corporate mergers and acquisitions.

Enterprise Transaction Gateway (ETG). An EDI gateway developed by CLT Appraisal Services and running on Windows NT which supports multiple messaging protocols and transaction formats.

entry page. The first page a visitor views when entering a Web site (surprising to many, the entry page is not always the home page). Compare exit page and path through site.

EPH Electronic Payment Handling. The banking system capabilities needed to support Echeck and capable of reducing bank costs. The logical providers of EPH are automated clearing houses

ESP. (See Encapsulating Security Payload.)

e-tailing. E-tailing refers to retailing over the internet. Thus an e-tailer is a B2C business that executes a transaction with the final consumer. E-tailers can be pure play businesses like Amazon.com or businesses that have evolved from a legacy business, Tesco.com. E-tailing is a subset of e-commerce.

Ethernet. Computers on the Internet that use the TCP/IP protocols are frequently connected to the Net over an Ethernet link. Ethernet supports communications at 10 mbps over several types of wiring. A type of network interface card that connects an individual computer to a network. See NIC.

eWallet. eWallet is a system that stores a customer's data for easy retrieval for online purchases. Since completing forms as part of an e-tail transaction can be a reason for aborting a transaction, an eWallet service can reduce this inconvenience for the consumer.

Excite. A popular Web portal until it went bankrupt last year. As a result, iWon, another popular Web portal, acquired the Excite Web property. IWon liked the brand so much they changed their company to the "The Excite Network."

exit page. The last Web page an individual user looks at on a given Web site. Common exit pages are often identified in the log file. A Web merchant or publisher may modify the most common exit pages in order to induce viewers to stay on the site for a longer time.

export law. A United States export law, administered by the Department of State, forbids the export of cryptography software or hardware using a key longer than forty bits without a permit. Export to subsidiaries of US companies is permitted. The law exists primarily to prevent hostile groups from encrypting messages which the US intelligence agencies (See National Security Agency) will have difficulty decrypting. With the increasing speed of computers forty bit cryptography is considered relatively weak and has, in fact, been broken. The cryptography industry is pressing the government to change the law so that US companies can export cryptography which is competitive worldwide. (See differential work factor cryptography.)

exposure. See impression.

Extensible Authentication Protocol. A framework for handling a variety of Point-to-Point Protocol authentication methods including cleartext, challenge/response, and arbitrary dialogue sequences.

Extensible Forms Description Language (XFDL). A protocol for creating and using legally binding Extensible Markup Language documents. The forms contain all the data, presentation, computational logic, and business semantics for a specific transaction and is signed digitally. XFDL may transform electronic data interchange (EDI) into a Web-based infrastructure.

Extensible Markup Language (XML). A document description language, primarily used to define Web pages and applications, that are compatible with Hypertext Markup Language (HTML) but provides more capabilities and flexibility. XML removes presentation constraints imposed by HTML and, in fact, does not necessarily require a Web browser. While both languages are platform independent, XML is also database and file format independent. To display an XML document (or run the XML application) the user's machine must be equipped with an XML parser. For basic XML documents, any XML parser can infer the document rules simply by the way the elements are presented. For more complicated documents or applications the author must develop or utilize a document-type definition (DTD) that defines the structure and rules for a given type of document. The XML parser refers to the DTD in order to determine how to display the document or run the application. More or less standard DTD's have been developed for engineering, law, medicine, and other areas of knowledge.

extranet. Extranet refers to a group of websites, belonging to independent entities that are combined together in order to share information. This is in contrast to an intranet, which is a private site that is only accessible for employees of an entity. Extranets are used in the supply chains to allow for more effective communications along the supply chain. They are replacing proprietary standard networks that are considerably more expensive to establish, and therefore were only used by large organizations.

FAQ. FAQ is an acronym for Frequently Asked Questions. An FAQ document is a document found on company web sites that addresses basic questions. These documents are updated from queries that come from the customers, so they *should* evolve over time.

FAST search. Search engine that powers the AllTheWeb search engine.

Favicon.ico (Favorite icon). Customized image that Microsoft Internet Explorer version 5.0 and above uses, if it is available, as an icon to go with a user-specified bookmarked site on the Links bar at the top of a Web browser window.

Favorites. Method of recording the address of a file or Web page for later reference in the Microsoft Internet Explorer browser.

FFA (Free For All). Links page where anyone can add a link. Do not bother with submitting your site to FFA pages, as it will only generate lots of spam emails for you, and very little traffic, if any at all.

fiber optics. A method of transmitting light beams along optical fibers. A light beam, such as that produced in a laser, can be modulated to carry information.

file compression. This makes computer data smaller so less is needed to represent the same information and, consequently, the information takes up less disk or file space and may be transmitted in less time.

file server. A file-storage device on a local area network (LAN) that is accessible to all users on the network. It is sophisticated, also serving as a manager of sorts, maintaining order as users request files and make changes to them.

filesharing. Filesharing refers to peer-to-peer technology that allows one user of the internet to access files of another user of the internet through a public directory. Before the advent of WWW, this was the primary form of internet information sharing, through public (and private) FTP sites. It has now emerged as a methodology for sharing digital files across the web. Napster pioneered this, distributing music files. Others, such as gnutella are proving to be interesting distribution models for music etc.

FIMAS. Financial Institution Message Authentication Standard. See X9.9.

FindWhat. A popular pay per click search engine supplying results for some of the most popular search and metasearch engines on the Internet, including InfoSpace, Excite, WebCrawler, NBCi, MetaCrawler, Dogpile, Go2Net, and CNET's Search.com.

finger. A program used to find out if someone is online — it may also reveal their full name and their plan and project files.

firewall. (1) A special computer or software application that is set up on a network to prevent intruders from stealing or destroying confidential files. (2) A computer that provides a defense between one network (inside the firewall) and another network (outside the firewall, such as the

Internet) that could pose a threat to the inside network. All traffic to and from the network must pass through the firewall. Only authorized traffic, as defined by the local security policy, is allowed to pass through the firewall, which is itself immune to penetration.

first-mover advantage. The First-Mover Advantage refers to the advantage gained by the first company that enters a certain market. This advantage is exacerbated for digital products and markets. There are a number of reasons this advantage exists. A company that is able to increase sales quickly is able to reduce the average cost of the product, over other competitors. This allows the first company to have more flexibility with pricing, either reducing the price to make it less attractive for new entrants (increasing barriers to entry) or increasing the margin and therefore profit while prices remain fixed, this additional profit can then be used for further innovation. The first-mover can also take advantage of the learning curve effect. First-mover advantage can be further successful if the company is able to achieve lock-in of its installed-base. Thus once lock-in occurs, it is more difficult for other marketers to attract those customers away from the first marketer.

First-mover advantage is not always sustainable, and Microsoft has been very effective at being the second company in many markets, and subsequently dominating those markets. A simple example of this was the Netscape's browser vs. Microsoft's Internet Explorer. Netscape was the first-mover, gaining upwards of 90% market-share, but was not able to sustain its position with the onslaught of Microsoft. Netscape did not establish ANY lock-in, either due to the user interface, or proprietary functionality and both products were essentially being given away, so there was no price advantage. Microsoft is clearly positioned to give a product away for the long-term to gain market share.

first-time visitor. A visitor to a Web site who has never visited the site before. See repeat visitor.

fixed costs. Fixed costs refer to the costs associated with a product, that are fixed over a number of units. Thus regardless of the number of units produced and sold, the fixed costs remain the same. Examples of fixed costs are rent on equipment, utility costs, and research and development costs. With digital products, much of the fixed costs are actually sunk costs, and therefore non-recoverable costs. A large portion of the costs associated with digital products are fixed, and sunk, and not variable costs, which are more typical of traditional manufactured goods. Break even analysis, which is a tool that determines the volume at which a company must sell a product in order to break even, distinguishes between fixed and variable costs in its calculations.

flame. To heap written abuse on someone or to excessively criticize them for their ideas, spelling, grammar, etc. Flaming is considered impolite, juvenile behavior, but is not uncommon in some newsgroups.

flame war. Exchange of angry, inflammatory, or insulting messages between Internet users.

Flash. Popular authoring software developed by Macromedia. It's used to design and deliver low-bandwidth animations, presentations, applications, and Web sites. To view a Flash file, users have to install the Macromedia Flash player.

flat file. A single file containing all the data on a particular subject.

flexibility of the communications medium. The flexibility of the communication's medium refers to its ability to serve multiple roles for the marketer. Media typically are restricted in terms of the types of transactions they can accomplish. TV is very good for reaching a large audience with a 30 second message, but is not useful for customer service. The web, however, is truly flexible. It can communicate information to multiple target audiences, simultaneously. It can provide and support customer service initiatives and it can be used to execute transactions. It is the first medium that can serve multiple roles simultaneously.

float. Money deposited in a customer's account that earns interest for the merchant.

follow-up. A reply to a Usenet posting.

footer. Often used to refer to the bottom part of a Web page.

forking. Forking refers to the notion that a project may evolve in multiple directions as multiple people have different goals for the project. This may occur under the open source development model. It is highly discouraged, as it does not maximize the use of resources. A good leader of an open source project will develop a process to try to avoid this situation.

frames. Allows you to present Web pages in multiple, independent windows or subwindows, where certain information can be kept visible, while content in the other windows are scrolled or replaced.

Free-Net. An open-access, community-sponsored and maintained computer network, affiliated with the National Public Telecomputing Network.

free-rider. The free-rider effect refers to the notion that noncontributors to a project can benefit from other people's work on the project. This effect is posed as a criticism of open source. The question is, does the free-rider effect negatively impact an open source project. Since free-riders do not actually diminish any resources as they use the product (open source software) and assuming they are not adding any additional burdon to the project (asking questions etc.) then the answer is no. For those who want to use the product, but need after sales service and customer support, a paid alternative may be available. (Red Hat for Linux is an example.)

The essay, Tragedy of the Commons, highlights the consequences of the free-rider issue when resources are finite. The argument is, the more people use the resource, the more the resource is depleated. Thus in this environment, we cannot afford free-riders, those not contributing to development of the resource. With an open source project, the opposite effect is true, as more developers work with the code, the better the product, and those not developing code (free-riders) have no negative impact on the code's development.

free software. Free Software is software that allows the owner the freedom to use the software, and alter the software in anyway he/she desires. Thus it is more akin to freedom of speech, rather than free as in zero cost (in fact, free software licenses can allow for the sale of free software under certain conditions). Free software development has evolved from the early hacker culture, where all software was free software. Free software is distributed with its source code. Access to this source code allows developers to improve and adapt the code for the individual use. Developers that do modify the code may be required (via the software's license) to submit any modifications back to the initiators of the project (submitting a patch). This allows any improvements, or resolved bugs, to be included in new releases of the product.

Free Software can include a license, explaining the rights of the developer and the usability for the owner of the copy. The GNU GPL license, designed by Richard Stallman and the FSF, has been very successful in developing a movement for the greater availability of free software. This free software is part of Richard Stallman's GNU project (Gnu's Not Unix).

In 1997 the term open source was developed with the thought of using this term to replace free software, as the free *implied* no cost, therefore not good work. Since this time, there has been a split in the free software movement camps, with the open source group (evangelized by Eric Raymond) promoting the business advantages of free software, and the free software camp promoting the ideological aspects of free software. The ideological aspects are that all software should be freely available, so developers can expand on each others work in order to continue the development process. Once code has been taken private, that innovation is lost to the public. Since that code will include previous "open" work (as would any work that has evolved from other work) it should also remain open. The freedom ideology works best if all software code is open, and does not tolerate free software and proprietary software as existing together. Once some code goes proprietary, the advantages of freedom are diluted, as free software development is now excluded from some development initiatives.

Of all the successes of the free software / open source movement, one can look at the GNU/Linux development.

frequency capping. Limiting the number of times a given advertisement is presented to the same person.

front-end. Application that Web users interact with directly. For example, a search form is the front-end of a search engine.

FTP (File Transfer Protocol). The principle of FTP is simple. You logon to a site (using your **FTP software**), then you choose a file to transfer. All FTP activity requires you to log on to the remote computer with a user name and password. To get to files shown on the map, it's important to understand the concept of *anonymous FTP*. Here, you log on to the machine as a guest rather than as an authorized account holder. In this situation, type "anonymous" as the user name and your full e-mail address as the password. Once you log on, you'll be able to access specified directories as an anonymous user. You can also access FTP sites with your Web browser. In the location or dialog box, type ftp://123.456.789.0 (using the appropriate IP address), or ftp://www.ftp.com (using the appropriate URL), and log on. From that point on, navigate through the site like you would a file directory on your computer.

FTP servers. Computers on the Internet that store files for transmission by FTP.

FYI (For Your Information). A subseries of RFCs that are not technical standards or descriptions of protocols. FYIs convey general information about subjects related to TCP/IP or the Internet.

g

game theory. Game Theory is a theory of rational behavior of participants in interactive decision-making scenarios. It helps predict how other participants of the situation/scenario (game) will respond in certain situations, or to certain decisions. Understanding participants' responses ahead of a decision, should help the initial decision maker make better decisions. It is applicable in areas such as:

— open source development. Freerider issues for example. Should you contribute resources when someone else may benefit without contribution?

— standards setting. Should you cooperate with your competitors to help expand and standardize the marketplace?

— dynamic pricing. Should you bid at a price point, and will that create a higher bid from someone else?

— competitor reactions to decisions. When making marketing decisions, you cannot only analyze how your customers may respond without considering how your competitors will respond, as this will in turn impact your customers.

A popular game theory model, for a non-zero sum situation, is the prisoners dilemma.

gateway. A computer that links two networks, routing IP datagrams and often converting protocols or messages from one network to the other. The term can also refer to a system capability that provides direct access to other remote networks or services.

gateway server. A firewall that filters traffic based on applications requested by clients on the trusted network.

Gbps (Gigabits per second). 1 Gbps = 1 billion bits per second. A measure of bandwidth on a digital data transmission medium such as optical fiber.

geek. A person who is proficient in one or more technical areas, especially in hands-on utilization of technology. At its most extreme geek implies a total lack of interest, ability, and even awareness of all aspects of life unrelated to technology.

Gibralter. Microsoft's original name for its Web server, now called the Internet Information Server.

GIF (Graphics Interchange Format). A file format developed by CompuServe Information Service (in 1987) for storing 256 color, raster (as opposed to vector) graphical images.

giga-. Prefix meaning one billion (1,000,000,000).

gigabit. In data communications, a gigabit is one billion (1,000,000,000) bits.

gigabyte. Measure of computer data storage capacity. One gigabyte is 1,073,741,824 bytes.

gigalapse. A massive denial of customer access to the Internet due to demand for services exceeding capacity. See xlapse.

global system for mobile communications (GMS). The standard for digital cellular phone service set by the European Telecommunications Standards Institute and used in Europe, Japan, Australia, and most countries outside the Americas.

GlobeSpan. A digital and analog transceiver chip set and technology from AT&T Paradyne that adds 6Mbps of bandwidth for asymmetrical digital subscriber line (ADSL) and high-bit rate digital subscriber line (HDSL) applications to a standard phone line for distances up to 18,000 feet. At a cost to a telco of $500 to $1,500 per line, GlobeSpan is intended to support simultaneous delivery of video, voice, and high speed data.

GMS. See global system for mobile communications.

go button. See button.

Google. The most widely used search engine in the World. It claims to be the World's most comprehensive search engine having indexed over 2.4 billion Web pages.

Gopher. A menu-based system that allows a user to access information from a remote computer. Menu items point to a file or directory item, which may be located on the same computer or on a different one. Gophers essentially point to other gophers on remote machines. Through gopher, you can telnet to remote computers and perform searches on searchable databases.

Graphical User Interface. A GUI (pronounced "gooey") is a graphics-based interface that lets you access programs by pointing to icons, buttons, and windows rather than by typing a string of commands at a command prompt.

gross exposures. Total number of times an ad is served, including duplicate downloads, to the same user.

group buying model. Group Buying Model refers to the notion that the internet allows individual consumers to develop a community and participate in purchases by multiple people with similar needs. TogetherWeSAVE.com is an example (Note: Mercata and Accompany closed, signalling this model is not yet matured!) Individuals are now able to take advantage of purchasing economies of scale that previously were only afforded to large companies. This in itself helps the power shift away from the company, to the individual consumer, but when combined with the reverse pricing model can create a potent consumer weapon. The essay, COMsumer Manifesto, details possible implications.

groupware. Groupware refers to technology that allows for groups of people to communicate from remote locations. The internet can be considered the ultimate open standard groupware technology! Applications typically included in groupware techology are calendars, discussion boards, project management tools, e-mail facilities etc. Microsoft Exchange and Lotus Notes are the more common commercial applications.

guerrilla marketing. Unconventional marketing techniques for achieving maximum results from minimal resources or budgets.

GUI (Graphical User Interface). Graphical (rather than purely textual) user interface to a computer.

h

hackers and crackers. Hackers is a term used for those who have been closely associated with the development of the computer, outside of the traditional corporate structure, and the free software movement (also known as the Open Source movement). Those that help develop code to improve (or create new) software, and share that code with fellow hackers. Hackers therefore **make** things. Crackers *break* things. They are those who get their thrills by cracking software, creating viruses, and destroying things. Unfortunately media often confuse the terms, thus the term hacker, when mentioned in mainstream media, usually refers to crackers!

The hacker philosophy is one of sharing, openness, and decentralization (a distinct disdain for bureaucracy), that helps the innovative process and increases the knowledge base of the culture. The hacker culture typically has an antagonistic relationship with the corporate entities who dominate the technology industry (this used to be IBM, and now Microsoft). Their values and belief systems are not aligned with these bureaucracies (who hoard knowledge and turn it into their selfish gain, rather than share knowledge and believe in the freedom of knowledge). Along these lines, hackers believe in the selflessness in favor of the common good. Communities of hackers can be found at sites like Slashdot.org.

Clearly this culture experiences network effects. The more people involved and contributing to a particular project, the more each person involved benefits from each others' innovations. This clearly answers the question as to how the Linux operating system was able to become a more robust operating system (according to some) than the Windows operating system, in a much shorter time frame.

Key figures in the hacker community are Richard Stallman (believes that all software should be free), Linus Torvalds (initiator and leader of the Linux development) and Eric Raymond (believes software should be free when it makes business sense).

hard copy. A physical document, usually text on paper. While additions to *E-commerce Dictionary* appear as soft copy in this Web page the original book is available in hard copy. (move to contact page for more information.)

Harvest. An architecture for searching for data on the Internet developed at the University of Colorado. The architecture combines information "gatherers" located on servers and information "brokers" which communicate with gatherers and other brokers in their search for information. Harvest uses far less network bandwidth and index space than other search architectures and can work with a variety of search engines and search protocols. See metadata.

hash algorithm. A security utility that mathematically combines every character in a message to create a fixed-length number (usually 128 bits in length) that is a condensation, or fingerprint, of the original message.

hash coding. The process used to calculate a number from a message.

hash value. The number that results when a message is hash encoded.

HCI (Human-Computer Interaction). Study of how humans interact with computer systems.

HDSL. See High Bit Rate Digital Subscriber Line.

headend. A central distribution point in a cable television network that typically serves tens of thousands to hundreds of thousands of homes. In a traditional cable TV network all communication was one way TV video and sound carried from the headend to the subscriber residences. Cable networks have been upgraded to carry data and voice as well as video, and to carry some traffic in both directions.

header. The header component of a web page comprises the title and the meta tags, both elements critical for marketing a web page online. A web page includes two components, the header and the body component. The body component includes the text that is visible to the user. By clicking the "view" and then the "source" option of the web browser, you can see the header and body tags for this document.

helper. A program used by a WWW browser to process files that the browser itself cannot, for example a sound file, JPEG image, MPEG movie, or a compressed file. Also known as a viewer.

helper applications. Additional software occasionally needed to help a Web browser program deal with an unusual file on the Internet. When an unusual file is downloaded, a helper application takes over for the Web browser to open and run the file. An example of a helper application is Netscape's "naplayer". It opens and plays sound files when they are encountered on the Internet.

HFC. See Hybrid Fiber/Coax.

hidden links. Invisible links. Usually used by search engine optimizers to add links from a home page or site map to doorway and hallway pages, so that search engines can crawl and index them, while keeping the links invisible to human visitors.

High Bit Rate Digital Subscriber Line (HDSL). A technology that supports high speed transmission of data over copper wires. See Digital Subscriber Line.

hits. Hits refer to the number of files served when users access a web page. Total hits for a page will therefore equal the number of times the page is accessed X the number of files included on a page. Thus a page that includes one graphic file will serve two files when it is accessed; the html file of the page, and the image file the page calls. This is a metric that is often misused when media quote the activity a web page receives. (To double the number of hits, simply double the number of files the page includes.) Better metrics include impressions and page views.

hollow PC. See Internet appliance.

home automation. The ability of products to communicate with each other over some medium within the home such as twisted pair, coaxial cable, radio frequency, infrared, spread spectrum, or powerline. Control applications include lighting, air conditioning, heating, overall energy management, security, watering, and entertainment. The three leading protocols for home automation are LonWorks, CEBus, and Smart House.

homepage. The homepage of a web site is the entry point to the site. It is the page that will usually have a web address (AKA URL) that ends with .com, .edu, .org, .gov or .cc (the 2 letter code for the country outside the USA). The actual filename, in the above scenarios, is index.html Users can create their own homepages that may be subsidiary to the above, and therefore use a subdirectory, but using index.html as the filename is still better (otherwise viewers can see the files in your directory by typing that filename with the file path). While the homepage is designed to be the entry point to a web site, designers cannot assume that all viewers will enter the web site by that page. It is important to consider all pages as potential entry points, and design all pages to market the site online (meta tags etc.) and for easy navigation to find the homepage.

hops. The number of hosts between two Internet connection computers.

host. A computer system that is the source of network services; also the site where you can hold an interactive session.

HotBot. A search portal that is part of the Terra Lycos Network, but operates as a separate search engine in its own right.

Hot Java. A World Wide Web browser capable of interpreting interactive applications, or "applets" programmed in Java.

house ads. Self promotional ads that replace unsold ad inventory.

HTML (Hyper Text Markup Language). A system of marking up, or tagging, a document so it can be published on the World Wide Web. An author incorporates HTML markup in his or her document to define the function (as distinct from the appearance) of different text elements. The appearance of these text elements is not defined at the authoring stage; instead, formatting is applied when a browser decides how it is going to display the text elements.

HTML banners. Banner ads that include HTML elements, such as interactive forms or pull-down menus.

HTTP (Hypertext Transfer Protocol). Protocol used by Web servers to deliver and receive information. Used to exchange text, graphic images, sound, video, and other multimedia files on the Web. All Web page addresses start with "http", although its use is often optional.

HTTPS (Secure Hypertext Transfer Protocol). A secure extension of HTTP. This extension securely encrypts and decrypts Web page requests. Whenever you pay for goods using a credit card on the Internet, HTTPS will be used to ensure your credit card details are secure.

Human Factors. Study of how humans behave psychologically and physically in relation to particular products, services, or environments.

Hybrid Fiber/Coax (HFC). Upgraded cable TV facilities which use fiber optic cable in the backbone and coaxial cable to connect to cable subscriber homes and businesses.

hybrid pricing. Pricing model based on a combination of a CPM (cost per impressions) pricing model and a performance based pricing model.

hyperlink. A link that connects you to other documents, other places within the same document, pictures or HTML pages. Think of a hyperlink as an invitation to visit another place. A simple click on the link will take you there.

hypermedia. An extension of the hypertext to include links to pictures, sound, video, and virtual reality.

hypertext. Hypertext refers to the connectivity between web documents, which is non-linear. Thus any part of the document (word or phrase) can launch another document, or another part of the same document via a hyperlink. In this example, the word web is hyperlinking to an explanation of the word.

HYTELNET. A program that provides an easily adaptable and fluid connection to a multitude of networked information resources, including library catalogs.

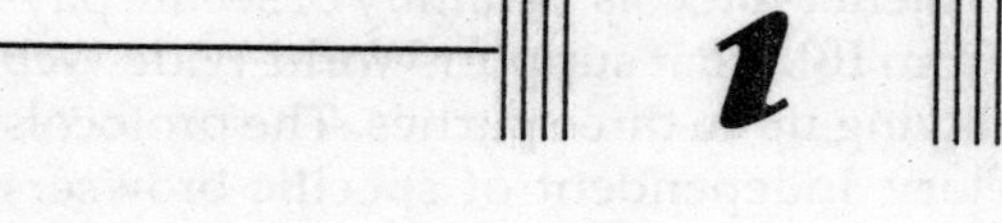

IAB (Interactive Advertising Bureau). An organization that fosters the growth of advertising on the Internet and recommends a set of standard size banner ads for Web pages.

IBEX. International Business Exchange. An online service that allows businesses to identify suppliers, make and receive bids, negotiate contracts, and arrange the delivery of goods and services world-wide. A company may post its requirements and receive bids without revealing its identity. IBEX is a joint effort of AT&T, Dun & Bradstreet, General Electric, and the U.S. Chamber of Commerce. It is scheduled for availability in 1996.

ICANN (Internet Corporation for Assigned Names and Numbers). A private non-profit corporation responsible for issuing IP address space allocation, domain name system management (.com, .net and .org).

ICQ ("I Seek You"). An popular instant messaging system that lets users exchange instant messages. It is generally recognized as being the first major instant messaging program available and is used by millions of users.

IETF (Internet Engineering Task Force). A voluntary group that investigates and resolves technical problems, as well as making recommendations to the IAB.

IFrame (Inline Frame). A floating frame that is inserted into a Web page.

IKMP. See Internet Key Management Protocol.

iKP. Internet Keyed Payment Protocols. A family of secure payment protocols from IBM that support World Wide Web transactions involving up to three parties. The protocols are non-proprietary, independent of specific browsers and servers, and exportable from the United States to most countries. They will support a wide variety of payment methods (e.g. credit cards, checks, smart cards). iKP does not provide encryption but supports other protocols which do (e.g. SSL, S-HTTP). iKP does require the provision of public keys by a certificate issuing authority.

ILEC. See incumbent local exchange carrier.

IM (Instant Messaging). A system that allows users exchange instant messages electronically (Internet, cellphones, WebTV, PDAs, etc.).

image maps. Graphic images that contain separate clickable areas.

IMHO (In My Humble Opinion). An acronym commonly used in IRC, e-mail and newsgroups. See IRC for more acronyms.

Immediate Response EDI. The use of EDI in exchanging messages among thousands of users to a central "online" application (e.g., dealers sending orders to a supplier and receiving a confirmation while their customer waits). The exchange is passed through directly between parties, not mailboxed.

impression. The delivery of a single ad (usually a banner) to a single viewer one time. Sometimes an impression is counted when the ad is requested (i.e. linked to) by a Web page and sometimes an impression is only counted when the ad is completely downloaded (and therefore has a higher probability of appearing on the user's screen before the user scrolls past the ad or moves on to a different Web page). Synonym: exposure. See ad serving system.

(page) impressions. Impressions refers to the number of times a page is accessed over a fixed period of time. Thus if a page receives 1,000 impressions per day, then that page is accessed 1,000 over the course of the day. This term is often confused with hits, which is actually an incorrect use of this term (hits and number of impressions would be the same if the page was simply a text page with no additional files associated with it). Page impressions also equals the number of times an advertising banner is served, assuming a banner is served each time the page is accessed.

incentivized traffic/clicks. Internet marketing concept whereby site visitors are paid to visit a Web site.

incoming links. Links going into a site from another site.

increasing returns. Increasing returns refers to the notion that the greater the size of the network, the greater the advantage of each participant of the network (network effects). Each participant of the network brings value to the overall network. This is in contrast to diminishing returns which refers to the greater the size (number of users) the less each participant can benefit from participation.

incumbent local exchange carrier (ILEC). The local telephone company, providing local service and connections to the

Public Switched Telephone Network to residences and businesses in its area.

index. A list containing every Web page found by a spider, crawler, or bot.

industrial revolution. This is the period of time that occurred after developments such as the steam combustion engine allowed for more efficient production of goods. The advent of the assembly line etc. occurred. It basically changed production from single goods to mass production. Mid 1800s to early 1930s.

Inferno. A crash project at AT&T Bell labs to develop a language to rival Java.

infoMarket. An IBM system which provides management of electronic rights over the Internet and IBM's Global Network using secure containers.

infomediaries. Infomediaries are channel intermediaries that are based on the transfer of information using the web. They are replacing traditional intermediaries in many distribution channels. Infomediaries include meta markets, portals, search engines, and bots.

Infosec Information Security. The preservation of the availability, utility, integrity, authenticity, confidentiality, and possession of information.

Inktomi. Provides search results to many of the major search engine portals and Web sites on the Internet.

inline image. On a Web page, an image that appears in the midst of text.

inline keying. A method of encryption and authentication that avoids setup overhead by inserting an extra header in every protected packet. See SKIP. In order to minimize the per-packet overhead, an inline keying header should be used only until the desired security association is established, at which point the peers will fall back to pure ESP.

installed-base. The installed-base refers to the customer base of digital products. The company will have records of these customers, and will be able to use these records in order to try to monetize the installed-base. Companies try to develop switching costs, in order to encourage their installed-base to remain loyal. By estimating the life-time value of a customer in the installed-base, we can estimate the value of the company.

instant messaging. Instant messaging is a form of synchronous communication that allows users, on a specific network (AOL Instant Messenger, ICQ.com and MSN Messenger for instance) to communicate with other users, on that network, by sending short messages. Instant messaging services also allow users to determine when other users are online. Given that users can only communicate with other users on the same network, these services are certainly good examples of services that take advantage of viral marketing. It is likely that, with time, these services may standardize, so users of one network will be able to communicate with users on another network. This model makes more sense, and is used for a similar service, text messenging on cell phones, common in countries outside the United States.

integrated POS terminal. A terminal at the point-of-sale, connected to a retailer's back office computer, that executes both point-of-sale functions and EFT-POS functions. It usually integrates an electronic cash register with a card reader and a PIN keypad.

integrity. The category of computer security that addresses the validity of data; confirmation that data have not been modified.

integrity violation. A security violation that occurs whenever a message is altered while in transit between sender and receiver.

intelligent agents. Intelligent Agents are "bots" designed to work for the user in terms of executing transactions (typically search queries at this point) across the web. It is assumed that as Intelligent Agents become more sophisticated, they can accomplish more complex tasks for their users. Once they understand their users' requirements, they can act somewhat independently of user interaction, in terms of making online purchasing decisions and other tasks that currently require significant search and user decision making processes. Intelligent Agents will also become more useful as industry standards are established.

interactive advertising. Interactive advertising is advertising that customers can interact with by sharing a mutual exchange of information and ideas.

interactive ad agencies. Ad agencies that use traditional print, broadcast and online advertising to get a message across.

interactive message access protocol (IMAP). A newer e-mail protocol with improvements over POP.

interactive multimedia. An application involving substantial user input or control and presenting at least two of the following: text, graphics, sound, image, video, and animation. Applications can be in the areas of education, entertainment, information and publishing, and transactions.

interchange. Fee that an acquirer pays to an association (or credit card company) to compensate the issuer for risks associated with accepting and funding the cardholder's account. This fee comes out of the discount rate charged to the merchant.

Intercast. A technology and open standard developed by Intel for transmitting World Wide Web pages at approximately 100Kbps in the vertical blanking interval of a standard television signal. While not supporting two way communication, Intercast will allow broadcasters and advertisers to provide text, graphics, and still images to home PC's. The technology requires a television receiver and a chip that converts the signal from analog to digital. Backed by PC manufacturers, broadcasters, online service providers and software developers, Intercast broadcasts are planned for nationwide availability in 1996.

intermercial. See interstitial.

Internet. The worldwide network of networks based on the TCP/IP protocol. A non-commercial, self-governing network devoted mostly to communication and research with roughly 20 million users worldwide. The Internet is not an online service and has no real central "hub." Rather, it is a collection of tens of thousands of networks, online services, and single-user components. Also, when not capitalized, *any* interconnected set of networks.

Internet access providers. Otherwise known as Internet service providers (ISP). These organizations allow other computer users to dial-in and connect to their Internet connection for a fee.

Internet Advertising Bureau (IAB). An association of companies that advertise on the Internet. Key activities include establishing terminology and standards for measuring advertising, conducting research relevant to electronic commerce and advertising, and addressing industry issues such as privacy and taxation.

Internet appliance. A computer designed to support client access to the Web (i.e. browsing) but without support for any popular PC operating systems or applications. Targeted to be substantially less expensive than a PC, some

Internet appliances will be able to use either a PC monitor or a TV for display. See NCOS.

Internet commerce. Another term for electronic commerce; sometimes used to refer to electronic commerce conducted on the Internet or World Wide Web instead of via private networks.

Internet Explorer. Microsoft's Web browser.

Internet host. A computer that is directly connected to the Internet.

Internet Key Management Protocol (IKMP). A part of the IETF standard for IPSec which combines the Oakley protocol for key exchange with the ISAKMP protocol for key management.

Internet Tax Freedom Act of 1998. A law passed by the U.S. Congress that placed a three-year moratorium on new taxes on Internet access fees and prohibited multiple and discriminatory taxes on electronic commerce. The Internet appears likely to drive a major simplification of the sales tax laws which vary greatly between different states and local governments across the country. The act also set up the Advisory Commission on Electronic Commerce.

Internet Transaction Broker. An alternative term for cybermediary created by Forrestor Research.

InterNIC (Internet Network Information Centre). (http://www.internic.net) For the United States, which is made up of three separate commercial organizations, and provides government-contracted services. This agency one of the primary official World Wide Web domain name registration services. InterNIC hosts a WHOIS service that you can use to see who a given domain name is registered to, or if that domain name is still in fact available.

InterNotes. A software product from Lotus Development Corporation which allows users to turn information into a database that can be accessed through the World Wide Web.

interstitial. A Web page not requested by a user, usually containing an advertisement, that appears on the user's screen, often in an automatically opened new browser, when the user has clicked on a link to move from one Web page to another. The page that the user originally requested continues to load and the interstitial is programmed to disappear after a few seconds or when the user clicks on it to acknowledge having seen it. Interstitials are interruptive, like television advertising, rather than passive, like Web banner advertising.

interstitial pages. Interstitial pages are a form of advertisement on the web that appears between web pages that the user requests. Thus when a user elects to enter or exit a website, a page appears with its advertisement, in place of the requested page, the user then needs to select from that page to receive the page requested (or the advertisement page will disappear after a fixed time). This is a form of interruption advertising (similar to broadcast models) but this form of web advertising breaks information design rules, as the user had a certain set of expectation when making the page selection, the interstitial page did not match the expectation. Interstitial advertisements are a form of web advertising, other forms include banner advertisements, pop-up advertisments, text advertisements and advertising buttons.

intranet. An Intranet is a network based on the internet TCP/IP open standard. An intranet belongs to an organization, and is designed to be accessible only by the organization's members, employees, or others with authorization. An intranet's Web site looks and act just like other Web sites, but has a firewall surrounding it to fend off unauthorized users. Intranets are used to share information. Secure intranets are much less expensive to build and manage than private, proprietary-standard networks.

inventory. Total number of ad impressions that a Web site or newsletter has available to sell over a given period of time.

invisible Web. Areas of the Web not indexed by search engines, such as database driven dynamically generated pages.

IO (Insertion order). Formal printed order to run an ad campaign. Typically, an ad space seller will send the advertiser an insertion order for them to sign and send back.

IP (Internet Protocol). Number 1 among the protocols upon which the Internet is based. IP allows a packet to travel through multiple networks on the way to its ultimate destination.

IP address. An IP address is a numerical address of the computer broken into 4 groups of 3 digit numbers lower than 254. In most cases, these addresses are unique for each internet connected computer throughout the world. Originally, addresses were obtained from Internet's Network Information Center (InterNIC) and later, in the Americas, the American Registry for Internet Numbers (ARIN). Today, only large ISPs are eligible to obtain addresses from ARIN, everyone else must request and address from their ISP. There is an exception to the uniqueness of addresses: Specific groups of addresses are set aside for use on internal networks for machines not connected to the internet or trying to conserve address space. These addresses are either 10.x.x.x, 172.16.x.x, or 192.168.x.x. Use of these addresses is becoming more popular due to the shortage of addresses, which makes individual addresses expensive to obtain and keep, and the costs associated with changing all network addresses when changing ISPs, and the popularity of internet connection sharing in small business or home networks.

As a web browser, we access a computer on the web by calling the domain name, which masks the IP address. Domain names are easier to recall. Domain names serve as the first part of the URL (web address).

IP address cloaking. The practice of serving search engine optimized pages to search engine spiders, while at the same time serving regular pages to site visitors.

IP Authentication Header (AH). A header that provides integrity and IP authentication without confidentiality to IP datagrams. The lack of confidentiality (which would require encryption) ensures that implementations of the Authentication Header will be widely available on the Internet, even in locations where the export, import, or use of encryption to provide confidentiality is regulated. The Authentication Header supports security between two or more hosts implementing AH, between two or more security gateways implementing AH, and between a host or gateway implementing AH and a set of hosts or gateways. For optimal security the Authentication Header should be used from origin to final destination rather than being implemented only in security gateways. All IPv6 hosts must implement the IP Authentication Header. IPv4 systems that claim to implement the Authentication Header must implement the IP Authentication Header. When implemented the IP Authentication Header must use MD5 with a 128-bit key or a stronger hash function. An implementation may support other authentication algorithms in addition to keyed MD5.

IPO. Initial Public Offering (IPO) refers to the offering of stock in a company to the public through a public market. NASDAQ is a popular market for e-commerce related companies. The IPO of a company serves as a significant liquidity opportunity for early investors, including founders and the Venture Capital investors.

IP telephony. Technology which supports voice, data, and video (both broadcast and interactive) over IP-based LANs and WANs and over the Internet. See Internet Protocol (IP), local area network (LAN), wide area network (WAN).

IP service. The carrying, for a fee, of data traffic using the Internet protocol. This is the essential service provided by Internet Service Providers and Network Service Providers.

IP-SEC. An IETF standard for encrypted sessions between corporate firewalls. DES with a 56-bit key is the mandatory encryption method. S/WAN is an industry standard implementation of IP-SEC.

IRC (Internet Relay Chat). A mechanism that allows for a number of Internet users to connect to the same network node and chat in real time. To access this feature, you need an IRC server.

Some IRC-unique communication acronyms:

AAMOF - As a matter of fact.
BBFN - Bye bye for now.
BTW - Back to work.
BYKT - But you know that.
CMIIW - Correct me if I'm wrong.
EOL - End of lecture.
FITB - Fill in the blank.
IAC - In any case.
IMHO - In my humble opinion.
LJBF - Let's just be friends.
LOL - Laugh out loud.
OIC - Oh, I see.
OTOH - On the other hand.
ROFL - Rolling on the floor laughing.

TIC - Tongue in cheek.
TTFN - Ta ta for now.
TYVM - Thank you very much.
<G> Grinning
<S> Smiling
<L> Laughing
<J> Joking

ISAKMP. Internet Security Association & Key Management Protocol. A leading candidate for Internet key management being considered by the IP Security Working Group of the IETF. ISAKMP provides a framework for authentication and encryption for many different key exchange methodologies. ISAKMP requires that at least one pair of messages be exchanged between the communicating peers before a secure link can be established.

ISAPI. Microsoft's proprietary API for interfacing between the company's Internet Information Server (Web server) and back-end services such as databases. ISAPI provides higher performance than the industry standard Common Gateway Interface.

ISDN (Integrated Services Digital Network). Special connections that use ordinary phone lines to transmit digital instead of analog signals. Briefly, ISDN is a telecommunications network that allows for digital voice, video, and data transmissions. ISDN replaces the slow and inefficient analog telephone system with a fast and efficient digital communications network. ISDN lines contain two channels: a B channel, which has a 64Kbps (kilobits per second) data transmission rate, and a D channel, which has either a 16Kbps or 64Kbps transmission rate. When the two lines are used together, transmitted data can travel at 128Kbps. Compare ISDN and T-1, T-3 lines.

ISO (International Organization for Standardization). An association that has defined a different set of network protocols, known as the ISO/OSI protocols, that are in line to replace those currently in use on the Internet. See also OSI.

ISOC (the Internet Society). A group made up of members who support a worldwide information network. It is also the governing body to which the IAB reports.

ISO Latin-1. An ISO code using 8 bits to specify 256 different characters. The first 128 correspond to the US-ASCII character set. The other 128 include control characters and characters common in European languages.

ISP (Internet Service Provider). An organization that lets users dial into its computers to connect to its Internet link for a fee. ISPs generally provide only an Internet connection, an electronic mail address, and maybe World Wide Web browsing software. You can use an ISP based in your town that offers an access number in your local calling area, or a national ISP that provides local-access numbers across the country (many of them also offer 1-800 dialing access). You can also connect to the Internet through a commercial online service, such as CompuServe or America Online. With this kind of connection, you get Internet access and the proprietary features offered by the online service, such as chat rooms and searchable databases. Internet access through online services may be more expensive than that obtained through an ISP.

ITB. See Internet Transaction Broker

IXC interexchange carrier. A company which carries long distance telephone traffic (e.g. AT&T or MCI.)

Ixquick. A metasearch engine that clusters its search results and ranks listings by the number of different search engines a listing achieves a top ten ranking, and the actual ranking it has received.

JANET (Joint Academic Network). The academic and research network in the United Kingdom.

Java. A programming language developed by Sun Microsystems to support widespread software distribution, particularly over the Web. It is a slimmed down and more secure version of the C++ programming language. Originally developed for use with set-top boxes, Java runs on Web servers and downloads small application programs, called applets, to Web browsers on an as needed basis. Because of strict built-in controls over software distribution the Java design protects against the delivery of incompatible software or viruses.

java applet. A Java application that runs on a browser.

JavaBeans. A software component model associated with the Java programming language. A JavaBean component is an object which can be used repeatedly by visually manipulating it into larger solutions. JavaBeans can range from low-level components, such as a scroll bar, to complete products like Corel's Office for Java.

java sandbox. A security model that confines Java applet actions to a security model-defined set of rules.

JavaScript. A cross-platform, Web-based scripting language that will allow a lay person to author HTML pages that use Java applets, objects, and classes without having to know how to program in Java. It can also be used to build standalone applications that can run on either clients or servers. JavaScript is being developed by Netscape and Sun Microsystems and is supported by approximately twenty-five other companies in competition with Microsoft's OLE and OCX's optimized for the Internet.

java servlet. An application that runs on a Web server and generates dynamic content.

JDBC Java Database Connectivity. A Java-enabled version of the Open Database Connectivity data-access specification. JDBC provides an API for developing data-access applets. The applets can then be downloaded from a Web browser to any database server with a JDBC driver. The specification was developed by Sun Microsystems and is supported by Oracle, Sybase, and Informix.

JPEG/JPG (Joint Photographic Experts Group). One of the two most common file formats for graphic images on the Web. The other is the GIF. JPEGs are typically photographic images. Files in this format end in ".jpg".

JTAPI. Java Telephony API A set of application programming interfaces that support interoperation between telephone switching equipment and a computer. JTAPI's principal advantage over TAPI developed by Microsoft is that JTAPI runs on a wide variety of processors.

Jughead. A program, used in conjunction with gopher, that provides the means to search all of the menu selections within a particular gopher server.

K/KB (kilobyte). Measure of computer memory or storage. One kilobyte is 1,024 bytes.

Kanoodle. A popular pay per click search engine Kanoodle supplying results for some of the most popular search and metasearch engines on the Internet, including AllTheWeb, AskJeeves, CNET.com, Dogpile.com, Lycos, NetZero, Mamma.com, MetaCrawler, and TurboFind.com.

Kbps (kilobits per second). In data communications, kilobits per second (thousands of bits per second) is the measure of how fast data flows on a given transmission path, such as an Internet connection.

key. a number used to encode or decode messages.

key library. A set of encrypted keys that belong to one person or that can be shared by a defined group of people. Access to a key library requires a separate key.

key recovery. While sometimes simply the process by which a key is retrieved from key escrow key recovery also refers to a substitute for the failed Clipper chip/Capstone initiative. In this scheme a copy of the key, in a separately encrypted key recovery field, is always sent along with the data which it encrypts. A predetermined private sector "Key Recover Center" can decrypt the key recovery field when requested by an authorized party (e.g. a government agency with a court order). A new cryptography export policy which took effect in late 1996 allows companies in the United States to export cryptographic algorithms using up to 56 bit keys if they agree to add a method for key recovery within their product within the next two years. Also see recovery key and TACDFIPSFKMI.

keyword. Keyword is the term used for words included in a web page that would match words used by web surfers in finding that web page (via a search engine). Keywords can simply be words included in the body text of the document, or added to the header using meta tags to increase the number of keywords. Selecting keywords, that match your target audiences' use of the web is a critical marketing tactic.

keyword density. The ratio of keywords contained within the total number of indexable words within a page.

keyword frequency. Number of times a keyword appears within a page.

keyword prominence. The importance of a keyword as determined by its position on a Web page. It's generally accepted that the closer your important keywords are to the top of the Web page, the better.

keyword proximity. Closeness between two or more keywords.

keyword stuffing. Repeating of keywords and keyword phrases in meta tags and elsewhere on a HTML page.

keyword tag. A HTML meta tag used to help define the important keywords of a page.

kilo-. Prefix meaning one thousand (1,000).

kilobit. In data communications, a kilobit is one thousand (1,000) bits.

knowbot. A registered trademark of the Corporation for National Research Initiatives. Knowbots are robots designed to seek out files on the Internet.

knowledge management. The intentional collection, classification, and dissemination of information about a company, its products, and its processes.

l

L2F. See Layer-2 Forwarding.

L2PT. See Layer Two Tunneling Protocol.

L2PT Access Concentrator (LAC). A device connected to one or more Public Switched Telephone Network or ISDN lines that supports both the PPP protocol and the L2PT protocol. It may tunnel any protocol carried within PPP and communicate with one or more L2PT Network Servers.

L2PT Network Server (LNS). A device that communicates with one or more L2PT Access Concentrators using the L2PT protocol and with only one LAN or WAN.

LAC. See L2PT Access Concentrator.

LAN (Local Area Network). A group of computers located in a relatively limited area (like an office building) and connected by a communications link that allows them to interact with each other. Many LANs are connected to the Internet.

last mile issue. The Last Mile issue refers to the connection between the user and the ISP, which is typically the slowest aspect of the internet access. As with a chain, the access is governed by the weakest link, thus the slow connection impacts the entire web browsing experience. This issue evolved due to the lack of competition in the telecom industry, until very recently. Therefore technology innovation was not as rapid (read *very* slow) compared to other innovations governed by Moore's Law. Users (in the U.S.) typically connect from home with a 56K modem. Cable modems and DSL technologies are beginning to become more widely adopted. Designers have to design for the web assuming users have a "slow" connection!

late outsourcing. The hiring of an external company to maintain an electronic commerce site that has been designed and developed by an internal information systems team.

Layer Two Tunneling Protocol (L2PT). A protocol that enables the tunneling of the data link layer of Point-to-Point Protocol between a remote access server that interfaces with dialup or ISDN circuits and a network access server that interfaces with a LAN or WAN. The L2PT protocol makes it possible to provide virtual dialup or support single user Virtual Private Networks over the Internet. L2PT does not provide encryption but will often be used in conjunction with encryption.

Layer-2 Forwarding (L2F). A capability developed by Cisco which is used in combination with the Point-to-Point Tunneling Protocol to provide the Layer-2 Tunneling Protocol.

LDAP (Lightweight Directory Access Protocol). A set of protocols for accessing information directories. LDAP resources.

learning curve. The learning curve represents the outcome of a company's experience when developing a product. As the company becomes more experienced, it is able to develop a better product, or develop products more efficiently at reduced cost. The learning curve effect has a significant role in helping companies benefit from first-mover advantage. Later entrants into the marketplace have a difficult time overcoming the experience advantage, as first-movers release additional versions of the product.

leased line. A dedicated (as opposed to a dial-up) telephone line typically used to link a moderate-sized local network to an Internet Service Provider.

LEC local exchange carrier. A company which provides local telephone service to homes and businesses within a given area (e.g. a Regional Bell Operating Company such as Pacific Bell).

legacy business. Legacy Business refers to a traditional business that develops a web presence to transact business. Barnes and Noble is an example. This is in contrast to a pure play business, which is developed as a new entity for the web, and had no prior presence, such as amazon.com.

lifetime value. Lifetime Value of the Customer determines the value of a customer to a firm, over the lifecycle of that customer. This removes the focus on individual transactions with customers and has become increasingly used with the developments of technology and market research, and thus the ability to focus on narrower target markets, even to the individual consumer in some cases. Lifetime Value is an important measure used for relationship marketing programs. Lifetime Value of Customers was a popular metric for internet firms as they built their customer bases.

In order to calculate the Lifetime Value, the company needs to determine the cost of customer acquisition, and the cost of customer retention, the average lifetime of a customer, and the average value the customer provides over the average lifetime. It is important to distinguish between customer acquisition and retention, as this will allow marketers to understand the true value of a specific marketing campaign (cost of acquisition), and the value new customers can bring over their lifecycle (value to company - cost of retention).

The Lifetime Value of the Customer = The revenue provided to the company by the customer over its lifetime - (Cost of Customer Acquisition + Cost of Customer Retention).

limited edition. A trial version of a software program; it can be used for free for a limited time period or for a certain number of uses.

link/hyperlink. Clickable connection from one word, picture, or information object to another.

link checkers. Software programs or online services used to check for broken links in a site.

link popularity. A measure of a site's popularity by the number and quality of links linking to a site.

link rot. Links to pages that used to work, but no longer work, because the page has moved or been deleted altogether.

link text. The text contained within a link.

Linux. Linux is an open source kernel developed by Linus Torvalds, and uses software tools developed by the GNU project to comprise an open source operating system. It mimics the Unix kernel, but was written from scratch with no proprietary code. Its development cycle has been relatively short (compared to the proprietary based Windows operating system) and is considered by *some* to be technically superior. Due to this, it has become the "poster child" for the open source community (it stimulated the interest of Eric Raymond and the paper Cathedral and Bazaar) and free software in general. While it is commonly referred to as Linux, others refer to it as GNU/ Linux (Richard Stallman) due to its reliance on other GNU software in order for it to function (more details here). Linux did prove to be the "missing link" for the GNU project by providing a usable operating system kernel, which has been packaged into a complete free software operating system by other hackers and commercial distributors (principal commercial distributors include Red Hat, Mandrake, SuSE, Debian (free software) and Slackware (one of the original hacker distributions)). GNUs efforts in this regard (the GNU Hurd) are still on going. Linux has wide adoption in the much smaller server side operating system market. Its penetration on the client side (where windows is dominant) has been limited to the hacker community.

list server. Program that manages email mailing lists and distributes new messages, newsletters, or other postings from the list's members to the entire list of subscribers.

LMDS. See Local Multipoint Distribution Service.

loading. The transfer of funds from a demand deposit account in a bank to an online account (e.g. a CyberCash demand deposit account) so that the funds can be sent over the net to another company or individual.

Local Multipoint Distribution Service (LMDS) A broadband wireless network that uses high frequencies (28 to 38 gigaherz) to transmit video and data to residences at less than a few miles distance.

lock-in. Lock-in refers to the ability of companies to ensure their customers do not switch to competitors, thus switching costs can establish lock-in. Switching costs can be established in many ways. The usability of a product can establish lock-in for that product, as customers learn how to use the product, they don't want to reinvest in learning how to use competing products. Wall Street Journal is a good example of trying to establish this type of lock-in. It heavily discounts its product to the education market, hoping that as people get used to getting their business information via the Journal, they will continue to do so after they graduate and begin working. The user interface of digital products are another example of this type of lock-in. The airlines establish lock-in by developing frequent flyer programs. As people fly more with one airline, the benefits they receive increase, in a non-linear fashion.

B2B markets, that increasingly rely on relationships and long term contracts are clearly prone to lock-in.

LOCT (Layered Open Crypto Toolkit). An RSA architecture which includes application specific tools, a certificate engine, cryptography engines, and a token interface. It makes it easy for application developers to use cryptography.

log file. A file created by a Web or proxy server that contains all of the information regarding visitor access and related activity on that server. Sample entries from an *Apache Common Log File,* (which just happens to be one of the more abbreviated types of Web log file; others, including Apache Extended Common Log File format, contain much more information):

111.222.333.123 - Jones [01/Feb/1998:01:08:39 -0800] "GET /bannerad/ad.htm HTTP/1.0" 200 198

111.222.333.123 - Jones [01/Feb/1998:01:08:46 -0800] "GET /bannerad/ad.htm HTTP/1.0" 200 28083

111.222.333.123 - Smith [01/Feb/1998:01:08:53 -0800] "GET /bannerad/ad7.gif HTTP/1.0" 200 9332

111.222.333.123 - Adams [01/Feb/1998:01:09:14 - 0800] "GET /bannerad/click.htm HTTP/1.0" 404 207

Description of Fields:

Field 1: User Address
IP or domain name of the user accessing the site.

Field 2: Domain (optional)
This field is used to log the domain for multi-homed web servers.

Field 3: User Authentication
Username of visitor who access the server

Field 4: Date/Time
Date and time the user accessed the site.

Field 5: GMT Offset
Number of hours from GMT (if this is +0000 it is logged in GMT time).

Field 6: Action
The particular operation of the hit (this must be in quotes).

Field 7: Return Code
The return code indicates whether or not the action was successful etc.

Field 8: Size
The size of the file sent.

logical security. The protection of assets using nonphysical means.

logic bomb. A malicious program similar to a virus except that it does not replicate itself.

login, logon. The process of identifying yourself to your computer or an online service. The initial identification procedure to gain access to a system as a legitimate user. The usual requirements are a valid user name (or user ID) and password.

logout, logoff. The concluding steps for formally ending a session with a system. Physically disconnecting or powering down a terminal does not necessarily result in a logout.

long domain names. Domain names that contain more than 26 characters. A limit of 67 characters, including the extension (.com, .net, etc.), is allowed.

LonWorks. A technology for control networks, including networks for home automation, developed by Echelon Corporation. Development time for network applications is greatly reduced by the implementation of the LonWorks architecture in integrated circuits available from Motorola and Toshiba.

LookSmart. A Web site directory that has a commercial search listings enabling businesses to reach 77 percent of U.S. Internet users.

lurking. A term used to describe the inactivity of a subscriber who doesn't actively participate in a mailing list or Usenet newsgroup discussions. One who lurks is just listening to the discussion. Lurking is advised for beginners who need to get up to speed on the history, mores, and etiquette of the group.

Lycos. A search portal that is part of the Terra Lycos Network.

lynx. A World Wide Web browser that displays only text. ch as Fed Wire.

macro virus. A virus that is transmitted or contained inside a downloadable file attachment; it can cause damage to a computer and reveal otherwise confidential information.

mail bomb. A security attack wherein many people (hundreds or thousands) each send a message to a particular address, exceeding the recipient's allowable mail limit and causing mail systems to malfunction.

mailing list. Electronic discussion groups that link a relatively small group of people together by common interests and that are distributed throughout the Internet via its global e-mail system. If you belong to a mailing list, you receive every message that is posted to that list.

mail reflector. A specialized address from which e-mail is automatically forwarded to a set of other addresses, commonly used to implement a mail discussion group.

mail server. Programs and hardware used to manage and store e-mail over the Internet.

Mamma. A metasearch engine that serves 7.9 million unique visitors, processes 30 million searches and generates 260 million impressions a month.

managed hosting. A Web hosting service in which the service provider manages the operation and oversight of all servers and assigns a dedicated service manager.

manual submission. Submitting a site to the search engines by hand, as opposed to automated software.

marginal costs. Marginal costs are the costs associated with creating an additional unit of product. This is similar to variable costs, which are the costs that increase directly with the increase in production (unlike fixed costs). Digital products typically have very low marginal costs, when compared with traditional goods (materials, labor etc.) and if the product is distributed via a web site, then the marginal costs can be zero. The consumer is bearing the distribution costs, and there are no packaging costs. This is why companies are able to market their products for free on their web sites, in order to try to entice further purchases at a later time (in the hopes of creating lock in perhaps). Netscape pioneered this approach and was able to offer its versions of its browser on its web site, changing the way software is marketed. This enabled them to create significant market share very quickly. They were able to do this, due to zero marginal costs.

marginal consumer. Marginal Consumer refers to the consumers that value the product least in terms of it satisfying their needs (the value proposition for the product is weakest among those that purchase the product). They are most likely to switch to other products to satisfy their needs, and will be the first in the marketplace to do so, if the marketplace changes in the favor of another product to satisfy the same needs.

market. A market traditionally referred to a place where buyers and sellers met to exchange goods. The exchange is a function of the positive sum relationship of the buyer and seller. A market is now better defined as a group of buyers and sellers for a particular product (a group of people who share a similar need). The advent of technology (industrial revolution) has seen the seperation of supply and consumption, hence the broader term for a market. The internet is now seeing the evolution of meta markets which represent a more traditional market viewpoint.

Types of markets include consumer (the exchange involves the final consumer, also known as B2C); business (exchange involves another organization, also known as B2B); global (exchange involves overseas parties); and government or non-profit. Each of these types of markets includes different marketing challenges, and thus different focuses within the marketing mix.

For markets to be effective, rules (legal framework) need to be established. Thus as emerging markets mature, and legal frameworks are better established, markets can become more vibrant.

marketing mix. A Marketing Mix is the combination of product offerings used to reach a target market for the organization. The marketing mix comprises the **Product** (what the actual offering comprises), **Price** (the value exchanged for that offering), **Promotion** (the means of communicating that offering to the target audience, promotional mix) and distribution (also known as **Place**, the means of having the product offering available to the target audience). The marketing mix is also known as the four Ps.

market segmentation. The method of identifying a group of consumers, within a broader market, that has similar characteristics and needs. Segments can be identified by examining demographic, psychographic, and behavioral differences. Thus a car manufacturer may identify different types of consumers preferring different styles of cars, so they will segment their car buying markets accordingly. Perhaps identifying that younger car buyers, with high incomes, will be more likely to buy a sports car, while an older population of car buyers may be more apt to purchase a town car. Once these segments are identified, marketers can develop different marketing mixes that target each segment. Again, the marketer may identify a number of specialty magazines that the young, affluent market reads, thus they will run their advertisements for sports cars in these magazines.

marketspace. A market that occurs in the virtual world instead of the real world.

mass individualization. The customizing of products for individual consumers on a large scale and at a low cost. It requires the consumer to participate in the individualization.

MB (megabyte). A measure of computer memory. One megabyte is 1,048,576 bytes or 8,388,608 bits.

Mbps (megabits per second). In data communications, megabits per second (millions of bits per second) is the measure of how fast data flows on a given transmission path, such as an Internet connection.

MCNS. See Multimedia Cable Network System.

M-Commerce. M-Commerce (Mobile Commerce) refers to access to the internet via a mobile device, such as a cell phone or a PDA. Once m-commerce becomes ubiquitous (it has greater rates of acceptance in places like Europe and Japan than it does in the US due to standards that have developed (Japan the standard is I-mode, in europe is WAP), it will change the utility of the web from a business standpoint. Contextual Marketing, the ability to communicate with a person when the person is likely to be receptive to the communication, will begin to occur, due to the mobility of access versus a PC. SMS is the messaging system across mobile devises that complements m-commerce.

medallion. The microchip within a smart card.

media brokers. People or companies that broker ad space between Web site owners and media planners and buyers.

media buy. The buying of advertising.

media buyers. People who place advertising orders by requesting proposals and negotiating the final cost.

media kit. Information file about a business or product.

media planners. People who deal with the planning of ad campaigns.

medium, media. Medium is the means of communication. Commonly referred to by its plural, media. Typical commercial media are TV, radio, newspapers and magazines. A piece of paper is also a medium, as it can carry a message, communicated between the sender (the author of the note/memo/story) and the receiver (those reading the content of the paper). The internet, and its various components are media.

The web, as a medium, is quite different to other, more traditional, media. It is a *distributed* medium, thus the content that the medium communicates originates from many (12 million, Jan 2001) web servers around the world. The web is a *non-linear* medium. Thus unlike other media, the consumer controls the navigation, due to the hypertext design. With other media, the marketer has more control on how the receiver receives the message. The web is a *multi-media* medium. This is in terms of its hyperlinking scheme, and its use of text, sound and video. If one considers various components of the web (chat rooms and discussion boards) and e-mail (actually an aspect of the internet, but enhanced by the web) then multi-media takes an additional meaning in terms of the types of communication it fosters. The web is a *niche* medium, it can satisfy the needs of those with obscure interests much like it can for those with mainstream interests. The web is an *unobtrusive* medium, thus users need to seek out the website, rather than having the web presence "pushed" to the consumer (obtrusive, like TV, radio, email etc.) The web is a *self-serve* medium. Consumers can use the web, when they want, in order to satisfy their informational needs.

mega-. Prefix meaning one million (1,000,000).

megabit. In data communications, a megabit is one million (1,000,000) bits.

merchants. Retailers who agree to accept credit cards, and have signed an agreement obliging them to meet requirements to do so.

merchant account. Account associated with a merchant. This account holds the money obtained through credit card sales until you transfer it to a different account. A merchant account is necessary for you to process credit cards.

Merchant Identification Number (MIDS). Unique number that identifies a merchant for reference and billing purposes.

merchant agreement. Contract between a merchant and a merchant account provider.

meta market. Meta Market is a web-based market centered around an event or an industry, rather than a single product. These are markets of complementary products that are closely related in the minds of consumers, but spread across different industries. The web allows us to match producers' desire for economies of scale, and consumers' desire for variety of choice to satisfy a set of needs. Thus we can have a meta market for a wedding (event) that includes honeymoon recommendations, sources for engagement rings and wedding gowns. Equally we can have a meta market for an entire industry (for example chemical industry) where the industry can trade excess inventory, source new suppliers and find new vendors. These types of markets are easier to establish in the web world, than they were before the web, and can prove very effective. Edmunds.com is an example of a meta market for the auto industry.

meta-message. In the EDIFACT standard, a message that describes the structure of other messages.

metadata. A description, usually in digital form and conforming to a well defined template, of a set of useful data. Also, an index composed of such descriptions. Analogous to a card in a library card catalogue system, a metadata description of a set of data might include an abstract of the data and the data's format, multimedia content, location, and usage fees. See USMARC, Harvest, WHOIS++, and Z39.50.

meta refresh. Coding on a Web page that automatically redirects a visitor to a new page after a specified number of seconds.

meta tags. Meta tags are tags that can be included in HTML source code in the header section. The most common meta tags allow the designer to include additional keywords into a document (keyword meta tag) and specify the text that appears when a search engine includes the document in its database (subject meta tag). They are therefore useful for increasing the utility of the document as it is cataloged by a search engine (for marketing purposes). If you click on the View option of your browser, and click on source, you can view these two meta tags for this dictionary.

meta tag generators. Software or online services that create meta tags based on input information.

MetaCrawler. A metasearch engine that now returns results from the Google search engine.

metasearch engines. Search engines that search a number of other search engines simultaneously, compile the results, and display them, either by search engine employed, or by clustering them together and eliminating duplicates.

metaspy search engines. Search engines that give you a glimpse of what other people are searching for, in real-time.

Metcalfe's Law. Metcalfe's Law states the number of possible cross-connections in a network grow as the square of the number of computers in the network increases. This is the law that governs network effects. The original quote, by Robert Metcalfe:

"The power of the network increases exponentially by the number of computers connected to it. Therefore, every computer added to the network both uses it as a resource while adding resources in a spiral of increasing value and choice."

MHz (Megahertz). Commonly used to express microprocessor clock speed. Most computers currently in use fall between 200 and 2000 MHz. In comparison, the first IBM PC operated at 4.77Mhz.

micropayments. Internet payments for items costing very little (usually 1 dollar or less).

microtransactions. Microtransactions are small transactions, perhaps of the order of a cent. They are being considered for digital content on the web (a magazine selling an article (unbundled) rather than an entire issue (bundled with additional information that may not be of interest to the consumer). This may then open up additional revenue streams for the content providers.

MIME (Multi-Purpose Internet Mail Extensions). System which allows a user to send audio, video, images, application programs, and other non-text information via email.

minimum bid. In an English auction, the price for an item at which the auctioning begins.

minimum bid increment. The amount by which one bid must exceed the previous bid.

MILNET. A part if the DDN network that makes up the Internet, centered on non-classified military communications.

MIME. (Multipurpose Internet Mail Extensions) Extensions to the Simple Mail Transfer Protocol (SMTP) that allow the transmittal of non-text information (graphics, etc.) via e-mail. A standard Internet format for encoding files that are attached to electronic (e-mail) messages.

mirror site. Exact copy of the original site on another Web server in order to reduce network traffic. It is usually updated frequently to ensure that it reflects the content of the original site.

modem (MOdulator/DEModulator). A device that allows a PC to communicate and exchange information with other modem-equipped computers via telephone lines.

moderator. Someone who presides over an online discussion forum.

Moore's Law. Moore's Law states that the cost of technology declines by 50% every 18 months. Gordon Moore, in 1965, observed that the number of transistors per square inch on integrated circuits had doubled every year since the integrated circuit was invented. In subsequent years, the pace slowed down a bit, but data density has doubled approximately every 18 months, and this is the current definition of Moore's Law, which Moore himself has blessed.

Mosaic. The World Wide Web client program developed by the National Center for Supercomputing Applications

(NCSA). It was essentially the first graphical WWW browser.

MOTO (Mail Order/Telephone Order). A card transaction where a merchant cannot see the card, for example, by telephone, by mail or on the Web. This is also known as a 'card not present' scenario.

mousetrapping. The use of browser tricks in an effort to keep a visitor captive at a site, often by disabling the "Back" button or generated repeated pop-up windows.

MP3. The file extension associated with MPEG audio layer 3 (MPEG-3). Layer 3 uses perceptual audio coding and psychoacoustic compression to remove redundant and irrelevant parts of a sound signal (parts the human ear doesn't hear anyway). The result is that MP3 music signals are compressed to a size $1/12^{th}$ the size of original with no noticeable loss of quality. (CD quality music is 1411.2 kilobits per one second of stereo music whereas MP3 music averages 112-128 kbps.) Because they are highly compressed, MP3 music files are easily transferred over the Internet, where they are traded regularly.

MPEG (Moving Picture Experts Group). Common file format for video files on the Web. Files in this format end in ".mpg" or ".mpeg".

MSN Search. Microsoft's search portal offering search results compiled from a variety of search engines and other resources.

MUD (Multi-User Dungeon). Modeled on the original Dungeons and Dragons game, it is a group of role-playing games that have been used as conferencing tools and educational tools.

multi-level marketing. Multi-level marketing (MLM) is a marketing scheme that rewards consumer resellers for the sale of the product and for the recruitment of other resellers for the product. Typically resellers are paid a commission on what they directly sell, and a smaller commission on their recruits' sales (and their recruits' recruits' sales etc.) This is the multi-level aspect of the term. Amway and Avon are the more recognized marketers that use this sales method. With the evolution of the web, we are seeing internet firms adopting this strategy with a viral marketing style program. Both viral marketing and MLM programs rely on the connectivity of consumers. Viral marketing programs do not offer an economic incentive to attract new customers, unlike MLM programs.

multimedia. Documents or platforms that combine different kids of data (plain text, video, graphics, audio).

Multimedia Cable Network System (MCNS). An industry consortium that defines the technical requirements for the interoperability of high speed cable modem and headend equipment.

mySQL. A free relational database management system (RDBMS) that uses Structured Query Language (SQL), the most popular language for adding, accessing, and processing data in a database.

n

name. A lexical string that is mapped to an IP address (e.g., *cutl.city.unisa.edu.au*).

name changing. A frowned-upon activity that occurs when someone purposely registers misspelled variations of well-known domain names. These variants sometimes lure consumers who make typographical errors when entering a URL. Compare spoofing.

name stealing. Theft of a Web site's name; occurs when someone, posing as a site's administrator, changes the ownership of the domain name assigned to the site to another site and owner.

NAS. See Network Access Server.

NAT. See network address translation

navigation. The actions of a user in exploring a Web site (or multiple Web sites) or in searching for information or resources. Also the design of a Web site, including links, text, graphics, and page layouts to facilitate navigation by users.

NCOS. Network Computer Operating System. An operating system from Oracle Corporation for use in Internet appliances. It will include electronic mail, videoconferencing, an Internet browser, and a rudimentary word processor.

NCSA (National Center for Supercomputing Applications). Hosted at the University of Illinois, Urbana-Champaign, the NCSA is one of the five original centers in the National Science Foundation's Supercomputer Centers Program. Mosaic, the first Internet browser program and predecessor to the Netscape browser, was invented at NCSA.

negative and positive spirals. These are events that reinforce each other, either positively or negatively, depending on the situation.

For a positive spiral, a positive event occurs, this triggers another positive event, this then has a positive effect on the first event etc. (known as increasing returns to scale). Thus if someone enters to participate in a network (purchases a fax machine) then that person increases the value of each fax machine in the network, since the fax machine is now more useful. This increased value encourages more people to purchase fax machines, which in turn increases the value of each fax machine, as a user can use it to communicate with more people. This is more commonly known as the fax effect, and while its example is a little dated, the concept still applies for growing networks.

A negative spiral occurs when simultaneous negative events impact each other. Thus as consumers leave the market place for a product, they can either decrease the value of the product for those remaining in the marketplace (this is common for digital (networked) products)) and / or increase the price of the product for the remaining consumers, as the average cost of the product increases. Either instance with have a further impact on the remaining consumers, and more consumers may therefore leave the market for the product, compounding the effect. Once this spiral occurs, many products will inevitably not survive. The Betamax standard is a good example of this.

NEST Novell Embedded Systems Technology. A Novell technology for transmitting data over power lines, currently at one or two megabits per second and eventually targeted to reach ten megabits per second. It lets developers run NetWare 4 on microprocessors (yet to be developed and embedded in home appliances) that are not powerful enough to support a typical network node.

net bandwidth. The actual speed information travels, taking into account all the traffic that may be on the communication channel at any given time.

netcasting. The broadcasting of information over the Internet using server push technology. Generally limited to webcasting.

Net Delivery Exposure (NDX). The time between when a cardholder is charged and when their order is successfully fulfilled.

netiquette. Netiquette refers to "internet etiquette." Since the internet does not have a set of rules established by a government, or an independent agency, it can (potentially) be a pretty chaotic environment. For such an environment to be effective, those participating need to follow the etiquette that is established. Thus netiquette refers to an established set of rules developed by the community itself, rather than an independent body. Since each participant of the internet has an incentive to see the internet prosper, we are more likely to want to follow netiquette to insure future growth of the internet, similar to the prisoners dilemma scenario. While as an individual, over the short term you may benefit from violating certain aspects on netiquette (defecting: using spam for example), in the long run, if everyone adopted such a philosophy, the internet would no longer be a useful medium, for anyone.

netizen. A citizen of cyberspace. An Internet user.

Netscape Scripting Language. A subset of Java, developed by Netscape, that comes with its own object library and does not permit users to create new classes of objects. It allows users to add functions such as forms processing to Netscape Navigator. See Java.

Netscape Search. Netscape's search portal offering search results from a number of popular search engines and other resources.

nettop. An alternate term for Internet appliance. Also see set-top box in the hard copy dictionary.

network. A group of computers connected together.

Network Access Points (NAPs). The four primary connection points for access to the Internet backbone in the United States.

network access providers. The four companies (Pacific Bell, Sprint, Ameritech, MFS Corporaton) that are primary providers of Internet access rights; they sell these rights to smaller Internet service providers.

Network Access Server (NAS). A device providing temporary, on-demand access by individuals to a network. NAS most commonly refers to a remote access server providing dial-up access over analog or ISDN telephone lines.

network address translation (NAT). The substitution of an official IP address for a private or unregistered IP address. NAT gives organizations more flexibility in assigning addresses internal to their network and allows users to share a limited number of registered IP addresses on an as needed basis. NAT is also used to make attacks(especially active attacks) on the network much more difficult by avoiding the transmission of internal IP addresses over the Internet as either source or destination addresses. NAT is usually performed by a router or firewall.

network computer. Oracle's name for Internet appliance.

networked economy. This refers to the fact that as consumers, we are now connected together, through the network of the internet. This increases the likelihood of consumers sharing information, as the cost of sharing information decreases and the means for doing so increases. This has a significant impact on the field of marketing and brand management. No longer do marketers control the messages they use to market their products to consumers. Consumers are now talking to each other and are becoming a viable source of information for other consumers. The viral marketing effect occurs due to a networked economy, as information is passed through networks at great speed. The connectivity that occurs in the market is enhanced as markets adopt specific communications standards. Once a standard has been adopted, the market can become more effective. Thus standards become very important in establishing a market and the subsequent success of the market in a networked economy.

network effects. Network effects refers to the notion that as more people participate in a network, the network becomes more valuable to each participant (a significant part of the value of the product/network, are the other participants of the network). This is also known as increasing returns to scale and a positive spiral. This effect is common in digital products, more specifically, products that benefit from the connectivity of the customer base. The fax has been used as a very good example of this. The first fax machine that was made available to the first consumer had no value to that consumer, since there was no one with whom to correspond. Once a second consumer owns a fax machine, each consumer has one person with whom he/she could communicate. When the third fax machine was sold, each owner could now communicate with two people, increasing the value of the product. This is known as the "fax effect" or Metcalfe's law.

Markets that experience network effects are prone to become more effective as more people join one network (product in the market) rather than having the market segmented with many proprietary networks (competitive market). Once network effects are established, markets tend to tip, favoring the market leader at the expense of other products in the marketplace. Thus, while we may not appreciate the dominant position that Microsoft has established in the software market (and they have behaved inappropriately as a function of this dominant position) there is no doubt that as consumers we are better off using software that each of us can transfer to each other when communicating with each other, and when moving from one organization to another (that may require employees to learn different software packages that accomplish the same tasks (different word processing packages etc.))

Network Service Provider. As opposed to Internet Service Providers who sell to end-users, Network Service Providers sell high volume Internet backbone capacity to Internet Service Providers. Network Service Providers often sell to end users as well. Sometimes called "carriers", Network Service Providers include MCI, AT&T, Sprint, and European Postal, Telegraph, and Telephone (PTT) agencies.

newsgroup. Collection of information and users who get together to communicate about one particular subject.

news readers. Programs that let you read and respond to messages in Usenet newsgroups.

newsletters/ezines. Electronic magazines delivered via email, or published on the Web.

news servers. Computers that receive, store, and serve Usenet newsgroup messages.

NFS (Network File System). Internet protocol used to share files among different hosts. A set of protocols that offers users access to other files on other networked computers as if they were local.

nic (Network Interface Card). The hardware that connects an individual computer to a network. See Ethernet.

NIC (Network Information Center). An electronic site where users can hunt down information about specific capabilities of a network. NICs are customarily maintained by regional networks and by institutions. The US national NIC is backed financially by the National Science Foundation, and is called the InterNIC.

NNTP (Network News Transfer Protocol). The Internet protocol used to transfer news using Usenet.

NOC (Network Operations Center). A site or group that is responsible for the daily care and maintenance of a network.

node. One computer (or other peripheral) within a network.

NREN (National Research and Education Network). A US attempt to link networks operated by different federal agencies into a single high-speed network.

NSAPI. Netscape's proprietary API for interfacing between the company's Web server and back-end services such as databases. NSAPI provides higher performance than the industry standard Common Gateway Interface.

NSFNet (National Science Foundation Network). Currently the Internet backbone network of the United States.

NSP. See Network Service Provider.

NTP (Network Time Protocol). A protocol used to synchronize time between computers on the Internet.

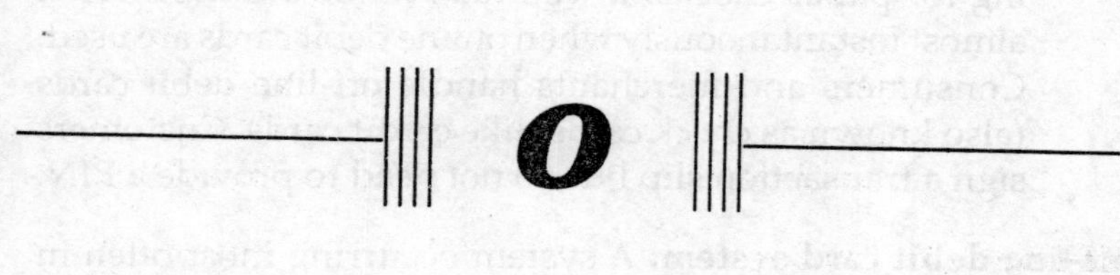

Oakley. A protocol for establishing session keys on Internet hosts and routers. Oakley provides perfect forward secrecy. It can be used with ISAKMP or by itself if attribute negotiation is not needed. Oakley describes a series of key exchanges - called "modes"— and details the services provided by each (e.g. perfect forward secrecy for keys, identity protection, and authentication).

octet. Alternative term for a set of eight bits (i.e., a byte).

OCX. Object Embedding and Linking Control. Microsoft utility programs which allow Microsoft's Web server software (See Blackbird) to link to other applications to present animation and other capabilities. Internet Explorer will be able to download OCXs and provide capabilities similar to Hot Java.

ODBC (Open Database Connectivity). A dynamic-link library (DLL) file that Microsoft Query and Microsoft Excel can use to connect to a particular database. Each database program, such as Microsoft Access or dBASE, or database management system, such as SQL Server, requires a different driver. ODBC drivers make Microsoft Query flexible, so that you can connect to new databases, as they become available, by installing new drivers.

offline/off-line. Not connected to a network.

off-line debit card. A debit card which settles transactions by drawing funds from the user's checking account approximately two days after the transaction - similar to the timing for paper checks. In contrast, funds are transferred almost instantaneously when online debit cards are used. Consumers and merchants handle off-line debit cards (also known as check cards) like credit cards. Customers sign a transaction slip but do not need to provide a PIN.

off-line debit card system. A system occurring most often in retailers handling small transactions (e.g. gas stations) in which debit card transactions are not validated and processed as they occur but are handled in batch mode. The merchant accepts the same risk of loss as with a paper check.

oil card. A credit card issued by a major oil company. See retail card.

OLE. Object Embedding and Linking. A set of protocols which allow programs operating in Microsoft Windows to cooperate with each other. An integral part of Microsoft Windows, OLE allows developers to use objects created in one application (such as charts created in Excel) in a document in another application (such as Word or PowerPoint).

one-sided tag. HTML tags that require only an opening tag (such as <P>, for new paragraph).

one-time password system. An authentication system in which the user's private key or pass-phrase is never sent over the network but is used to calculate passwords which are unique to the user and which are different and unpredictable each time they are used. One-time password systems are designed to protect against passive attacks by preventing replay of passwords that have been captured by eavesdropping on the network. IETF Request for Comment 1938 proposes a standard for one time passwords which is derived from S/Key.

online. Refers to the successful connection with another computer via telephone lines or through a network.

online broker. A retail securities broker that either provides all its services over the Internet (e.g. E*TRADE) or is an important competitor for online brokerage business (e.g. Charles Schwab).

online community. Synonymous with virtual community, which is an electronic gathering place for people with common interests.

online service. A dial-up service that provides news, information, and discussion forums for users with modem-equipped PCs and the access software provided by the service. (Examples include: America Online, Prodigy, CompuServe, Genie, Delphi, and Global Network Navigator.)

open auction. An auction in which bids are publicly announced.

open database connectivity (ODBC). A database protocol that makes it possible for a program to access data from an application, regardless of which database management system is dispensing the data.

Open Directory Project/Dmoz. The largest human-edited Web directory with over 3 million reviewed Web sites.

Open EDI. A model for EDI in which trading partners' applications exchange information with no prior human agreement required. It requires the use of an existing "scenario" developed by a user community. Open EDI will lower the barriers to establishing EDI relationships with new partners and facilitate the relationships between existing partners. The model is being developed by the international standardization committee ISO/IEC JTC1 SC30. CD 14662 is the draft standard.

open source. Open Source is a term, developed in 1997, to represent free software. The term was designed to emphasize the freedom of use aspect of the software (source code is open), and not allow people to assume free meant no cost (which it did not). Aside from the marketing aspect of the new term, there are also differences in the ideologies of the proponents of the open source movement as a "branch" of the free software movement. The open source movement (Eric Raymond et al.) believes that open source should be a business choice, and only appropriate when it makes business sense (Magic Cauldron paper discusses this). The free software movement (evangelized by Richard Stallman) believes that all software should be free, and only if all software is free will free software be truly effective. Since all software development relies on previous "knowledge", and that previous knowledge is public domain, then new knowledge, as a derivitive, should also be free.

While Open Source software must have a no-cost alternative (for it to comply with the open source definition) a marketer can sell a version at a price. (Red Hat's version of the Linux operating System is a great example.) The software releases are done so with the source code, which allows the consumer/user to modify the code for its specific purpose. Users that do modify the code are asked (via the license) to submit any modifications back to the initiators of the project (submitting a patch). This allows any improvements, or resolved bugs, to be included in new releases of the product.

The most important developments thus far in the open source and free software movement has been the evolution of the Linux operating system, began in 1991, and the announcement of Netscape's Mozilla project, in 1997.

open video system. A business model for distribution of video signals, established and regulated by the Telecommunications Act of 1996, in which an LEC may control up to a third of a video distribution system capacity and provide the remainder on a non-discriminatory basis to any and all content providers. An LEC operating within this model is not regulated as a cable TV system and is not required to obtain a cable TV franchise from the local community.

opportunity costs. Opportunity costs refer to the costs associated with giving up an opportunity. They are relevant in the marketing of digital products when one considers the value lost to the company when giving away a product for free. Since digital goods primarily consist of fixed costs and often have zero marginal costs then marketing strategy often dictates to give-away a version of the product to encourage consumers to upgrade at a later time (assuming lock-in etc.) The only cost incurred here would be the opportunity cost of the lost revenue from the consumers that would have paid for this version of the product in the first place. To avoid this situation, companies typically segment their markets, and offer a free product, with limited functionality (and no customer support or documentation) to a casual user group, and an upgraded version, at a price, with customer support etc. to a more sophisticated customer. The company will hope the casual user will upgrade to the upgraded version as they become more sophisticated users and more reliant on the product. They also assume the sophisticated user will not be satisfied with the free version, due to its lack of functionality

opt-in. The express act by a customer of granting a marketer permission to deliver marketing messages to the customer. The permission is typically granted by registering on a Web site or responding to an unsolicited E-mail and the messages are typically delivered by E-mail. See opt-out and permission marketing.

opt-in e-mail. The practice of sending e-mail messages to people who have requested information on a particular topic or about a specific product.

opt-out. The instruction by a customer to a marketer to halt the delivery of marketing messages, typically periodic E-mails. Most responsible marketers embed opt-out procedures in their marketing messages and make it easy for customers to opt-out. See opt-in and permission marketing.

opt-out email. Opt-out email is similar to opt-in email, except that the email recipient is automatically added to a mailing list, as they did not request **not** to be subscribed.

ORA. Organizational registration authority An organization which does not issue digital certificates but registers users and vouches for their identity to a certificate authority.

Orange Book. A standard published by the Department of Defense to classify computer security into four hierarchical divisions (A thru D) to specify the level of trust required by the U.S. government for particular applications.

OS (Operating System). Program that provides the basic functionality of a computer. For example, Windows, MacOS and Linux are all operating systems.

OSI (Open Systems Interconnect). A conceptual model and set of protocols for networks, promulgated by the ISO.

Other Digital Subscriber Line (xDSL). The entire family of DSL technology supporting data rates from 128 Kbps to 52 Mbps over various distances between the subscriber and the telephone company central office.

OTP. See one-time password system.

out of the box. Synonym for "off the shelf," meaning a ready-made software, hardware, or combination package.

outgoing links. Links leading out of a site to another site.

outsourcing. The hiring of another company to perform design, implementation, or operational tasks for an information systems project.

Overture. Overture, formerly known as GoTo, is the most widely used pay per click search engine. Overture supplies results for some of the most popular search engines and search portals, including AltaVista, GO, HotBot, iWon, Lycos, MSN Search and NBCi.

P2P (Peer-to-Peer). Process whereby computers can trade information between each other without having to pass the information through a centrally controlled server as with email or IM programs.

PAC. See PPTP Access Concentrator.

packet. A unit of data of standardized size, into which information is divided for transmission over a network. Each of the packets that comprise a message travels the internetwork independently; the message is reassembled from its component packets at the destination.

packet authentication. User authentication plus assurance of data integrity. Within the context of IPSec authentication means packet authentication and assures the recipient of an IP packet not only that the sender is who he or she claims to be but also that the data has not been modified in any way during transmission. Within the general context of gaining access to networks and resources authentication assures the identity of the user without assuring data integrity.

packet filter firewall. A firewall that examines all data flowing back and forth between a trusted network and the Internet.

packet switching. A message delivery technique in which information is broken down into small units (packets) and then relayed through stations in a computer network along the best route available between the source and the destination.

page jacking/pagejacking. The theft of original content from a site for republication at another site.

page view. A unit for measuring Web site readership which corresponds to one person viewing one page, or at least a portion of a page, one time. If a person leaves a certain page and returns to it in the same visit to the Web site two page views are counted. Page views are a more difficult to measure than hits but are a much more useful and relevant measure of the attention a page garners from viewers.

Paid Inclusion Listings. Guaranteed indexing of one or more Web pages by search engines or Web directories, in exchange for a fee.

Paperwork Reduction Act of 1995. An act that requires all federal agencies to use electronic filing forms to reduce demands on the public for paperwork 10% by 1996/97 and 5% annually through the year 2000.

partial URL. A Uniform Resource Locator which refers to locations in relation to the document currently being viewed, typically a location on the same server or Web site.

partner program. See affiliate program.

pass-along rate. The number or percentage of people who pass on a message or file, which is typically a measure of the effectiveness of word-of-mouth marketing.

passive attack. An attempt to break security by capturing information without altering it. See active attack, one-time password sytem, and replay attack.

patch. A patch is an addition to a piece of program, used either to repair the software (fix a bug), or submitted for inclusion in updated versions in the case of open source software.

path through site. The page-to-page course (path) a visitor takes through a Web site from the entry page to the exit page. See entry page and exit page.

payment switch. A network service, provided on Web servers from Open Market, that authorizes and executes digital payment orders over the Internet which are backed by external accounts. The switch creates digital representations of conventional negotiable instruments (e.g. checks, drafts, notes, bonds) and forwards them to conventional financial institutions. The payment switch uses "payment URLs" to enable purchases over the World Wide Web. Once payment is assured, the switch sends an "access URL" to the buyer that confirms the purchase of an item to be delivered off-line or enables the delivery of an online product or service.

payment threshold. The minimum accumulated commission an affiliate must earn to trigger payment from an affiliate program.

payment URL. A URL used by a payment switch that specifies a merchant, the name of merchant's payment switch, the URL of the product being bought if it is a product which can be delivered online, the price, the expiration date of the price/offer, and the digital signature of the payment URL derived from the merchant's private key. The switch combines the payment URL with the encrypted buyer identification and password or passwords. After authentication of the buyer and the merchant, the switch authorizes payment by the buyer designated financial institution.

pay-per-click. The ability to pay, typically in very small amounts or micro-payments, for information or entertainment received over the Internet or the Web. The term implies that each payment is automatic and that simply requesting the information provides agreement to pay for it.

Pay Per Click advertising. A form of online advertising whereby advertisers pay for each visitor sent by a search engine. Also known as Bid For Location, Bid For Position, Cost Per Click (CPC), Pay For Performance, Pay Per Performance, Pay For Placement, Pay Per Placement, Pay For Position, Pay Per Position, Pay For Ranking, Pay Per Ranking and Pay For Result advertising.

Pay Per Click Search Engine (PPCSE). A search engine that charges advertisers a fee for each click through the advertiser receives. Rankings are based on an auction system, whereby the the highest bidder is ranked the highest.

PCMCIA, PCMCIA card (Personal Computer Memory Card International Association). Credit card-sized plug-in boards for laptop and other computers. PCMCIA cards are used to add LAN adapters, modems, memory, storage and more.

PCT. Private Communication Technology. A mechanism developed by Microsoft and Visa to compete with Netscape's SSL in enabling spontaneous, flexible, and secure commercial transactions. Microsoft's STT builds upon PCT and is intended for end-to-end banking systems.

PDA (Personal Digital Assistant). A term for any small mobile hand-held device that provides computing and information storage and retrieval capabilities. These include schedulers, calendars and address books.

PDF (Portable Document Format). Adobe's PDF is a file format that captures all the elements of a printed document as an electronic image that you can view, navigate, print, or send. To view PDF files, you need the free Acrobat Reader browser plugin. Once you've downloaded the Reader, it will start automatically whenever you want to download a PDF file.

peer-to-peer. Peer-to-peer refers to the design of a service that does not rely on centralized networking services such as DNS to connect end users' computers and accounts for the unpredictable accessibility of these end nodes in making connections between users. Traditional networks follow a spoke-and-wheel design, where the network is organized around a central hub, the site's users come to interact with that hub from client workstations. In peer-to-peer applications, many or all of the functions performed in connecting a traditional, server-based network are off-loaded to the client machines connected to the network.

Filesharing is a clear use of peer-to-peer technology. It takes advantage of the end users' storage and retrieval capabilities across individual networks that includes other users of a filesharing system (for example, the gnutella network).

Think of a WWW model being a 24-hr shopping mall. The stores are web sites. They are always there. You can always go to the same place to find the same items. Peer-to-peer is more of a bazaar where the vendors come and go as they please. You never know what you'll find until you get there. The products aren't in the same place every time. All these wondering gypsies could pack up and leave town tomorrow and you'd be out there in the mall again, trying to track down where they went so you could go, too.

PEM (Privacy Enhanced Mail). A encryption standard generally used to secure Internet mail.

Perfect Forward Secrecy (PFS). An attribute of some encryption methodologies which assures that compromise of a single key will permit access to only data protected by that key. For PFS to exist the key used to protect transmission of data must not be used to derive any additional keys, and if the key used to protect transmission of data was derived from some other keying material, that material must not be used to derive any more keys.

perl. Practical Extraction and Reporting Language. A popular scripting language for writing CGI applications because it facilitates data and text manipulation.

permission based marketing. The sending of multiple marketing messages, typically E-mail messages, to individuals who have given the marketer permission to send the messages to the individual. The messages are often embedded in free E-mail newsletters that provide news and information. See opt-in and opt-out.

permission marketing. Permission Marketing refers to a communications process, between the marketer and the consumer, that the consumer gave "permission" to the marketer to participate. This is becoming more common with the web, as consumers "opt-in" to a mailing list from a company's web-site. This allows the marketer to develop an ongoing dialog, in order to build a positive relationship and communicate messages relevant to the marketer's product. Product information, combined with additional incentives (prizes or other rewards) are usually used. Seth Godin has pioneered this area.

persistent cookies. Cookies which remain on the user's hard drive until the user deletes it.

personal information number (PIN). A random assemblage of digits, chosen by the customer, that serves as a password for monetary transactions.

PFS. See Perfect Forward Secrecy

PGP (Pretty Good Privacy). A program used to encrypt and decrypt email over the Internet. It is also used to send an encrypted digital signature that lets the receiver verify the sender's identity and know that the message was not changed en route.

PICS. Platform for Internet Content Selection. A set of protocols developed by the World Wide Web consortium for communicating a rating for a Web, FTP or newsgroup server to an Internet client. PICS is intended to give users a method for categorizing, rating, and filtering Web and other Internet content. The protocols are extensions to both HTTP and HTML and allow users to customize selection criteria, or adopt, from a third party such as a Parent Teacher Association, established selection criteria or a list of sites to be screened out.

ping (Packet Internet or Inter-Network Groper). Basic Internet program that lets you verify that a particular IP address exists and can accept requests.

pixel. A single illuminated dot on a computer monitor.

PKCS #11. See Cryptoki.

PKI Public Key Infrastructure. A set of independent services to be developed by competing organizations that will support the use of Public Key in information security applications as well as in electronic commerce. The PKI will determine the policies for issuance of digital certificates, will issue and revoke certificates, and will save the information needed to subsequently validate the certificates. It will include certificate authorities organized both in hierarchies and in peer-to-peer networks.

plain old telephone service (POTS). The network connecting telephones; it provides a reliable data transmission bandwidth of about 56Kbps.

platform. A platform is an environment needed to run a piece of software. Thus the Windows Operating System serves as a platform for the Windows Office Suite. Further a browser would be considered a platform that a plug-in would need for it to function (thus Internet Explorer is a platform for Windows Media Player and Real Networks).

plug-in. Plug-in refers to additional software that is required to execute a transaction via a web browser. Thus if the webpage is designed to run with something that is not standard to the browser, the viewer needs to down load an additional plug-in. This may be used to run enhanced graphics (Flash), sound (Real Audio) or 3D (Cosmo Player), or other such rich media applications. Before designing to require a plug-in, it is important to note how much of your target audience has the additional plug-in, the likelihood of those not having the plug-in down loading it, and whether the design functions without the plug-in (i.e. does the additional feature(s) compliment or replace the information design of the site). As the web browser develops, the requirements of use of plug-ins will diminish, so this is a temporary situation. It is advised not to require the use of plug-ins on the homepage, especially if the information from the plug-in is required to meet the informational goals of the site.

PNS. See PPTP Network Server.

Point-to-Point Tunneling Protocol (PPTP). A call-control and management protocol that allows a PPTP Network Server to control access by dial-in circuit switched calls received by a PPTP Access Concentrator. It provides flow and congestion controlled encapsulation datagram service for carrying Point-to-Point Protocol packets. While PPTP does not provide encryption it can be used in conjunction with encryption to provide a Virtual Private Network over the Internet between an individual dialup user and a LAN or WAN.

policy card. A hardware device used in conjunction with an encryption engine to establish the strength of the encryption algorithm in a given computer. Policy cards could be adapted to support key escrow.

POP (Post Office Protocol). System whereby email is received and held for you by your Internet server. Any mail stored in your mail-box on the server can be downloaded into an email program.

POP (Point of Presence). Used in the context of telecommunications between companies and ISPs.

pop-under window. A new browser window that appears under the current browser window to display another Web page or advertisement.

pop-up advertisements. Pop-up advertisements are a form of web advertisements (like banner advertisements, interstitial pages, text advertisements, and buttons) that appear in a seperate window, either as a full screen (but behind the current window, and also known as a Pop-under ad.) or partial screen (over laying the current window). These advertisements, similar to some interstitial advertisements, do require the user to take some form of action (even if it is to simply close the window). The benefits are the user can simply continue to browse the web without being interrupted, yet still engage an action with the advertisement if desired, at a later time (unlike other forms of web advertising). Balancing this, they do create another window in the user's screen, that the user did not request, this can be considered somewhat annoying.

pop-up window. A new browser window that appears on top of the current browser window to display another Web page or advertisement.

port. A point of I/O access to a computer or system. Also, to convert a program from one platform to run on another (e.g., from Unix to MS-DOS or MacOS).

portable. Portable refers to the ease of mobility of the medium. A portable medium is one that can be carried with the consumer, wherever the consumer is. Newspapers and magazines are more portable that the TV or the web, the radio falls between the extremes. As the web becomes wireless, its portability (and hence utility) will increase.

portal. A Web site that provides at least three essential functions: a search engine, Web-based E-mail, and personalized news. A portal is intended to be the site its users first connect to whenever they log onto the Internet. It attracts users by providing personalized and customized services (E-mail and news) and providing search and directory services which are frequently used to find and access other sites. Some portals are provided to their customers by Internet Service Providers to make their service more competitive. Most portals gain revenue by selling advertising space on their sites.

port number (or port address). To ensure that each server application responds only to requests and communications from appropriate clients, each server is assigned a port address. If IP addresses are like street addresses, then ports can be thought of as apartment or suite numbers.

positive sum relationship. A positive sum relationship is a relationship between two entities which are, as a sum, better off from the participation of that relationship. This is in contrast to a zero sum relationship, where the outcome of the relationship is a gain for one participant at the direct expense of the other. Examples of positive sum relationships can be found in business transactions (trade in general) and in biology (bumblebee and the flower). Long term positive sum relationships are also known as symbiotic relationships. Zero sum relationships can also been seen in biology (the food chain) and in games, such as chess and checkers. Game Theory tries to predict best decision making outcomes based on the relationships of participants, and the consequence of decisions based on positive sum relationships or zero sum relationships.

PPA (Pay-Per-Action). Commission paid by an advertiser for a specific action generated by an affiliate.

PPC (Pay-Per-Click). Commission paid by an advertiser for each click through generated by an affiliate.

PPL (Pay-Per-Lead). Commission paid by an advertiser for each sales lead generated by an affiliate.

PPP (Point-to-Point Protocol). One way computers can communicate with each other over the Internet (compare "SLIP"). PPP connections let you communicate directly with other computers on the network using TCP/IP connections.

PPS (Pay-Per-Sale). Commission paid by an advertiser for each sale generated by an affiliate.

PPTP. See Point-to-Point Tunneling Protocol.

PPTP Access Concentrator (PAC). A Network Access Server capable of supporting the Point-to-Point protocol on one or more analog or ISDN lines and supporting the PPTP protocol to communicate with one or more PPTP Network Servers using TCP/IP.

PPTP Network Server (PNS). A device which provides the interface between the Point-to-Point Protocol (encapsulated in the PPTP protocol) and a LAN or WAN. The PNS uses the PPTP protocol to support tunneling between a PPTP Access Concentrator and the PNS. As described in an IETF draft document on PPTP, a PNS is expected to run on a general purpose computing/server platform. See Point-to-Point Tunneling Protocol.

PPTP Point-to-Point Tunneling. A protocol for use with remote access which carries encrypted, secure traffic over the Internet between an Internet service provider (ISP) and a remote access server. It requires the use of the Point-to-Point Protocol (PPP) between the remote client and the ISP and provides substantial savings versus telephone calls between the client and the remote access server using regular long distance or 800 number service.

pre-money valuation. Pre-Money Valuation refers to the value of the company before an outside investment is made. Thus if a company has a pre-money valuation of $5 million, and a Venture Capitalist invests $10 million, then the Venture Capital firm will own 66% of the business after the investment ($10M / $15M = 66%)

presentment. Demand for payment of a negotiable instrument (e.g. a check).

prisoners dilemma. Prisoners Dilemma is a popular game theory model. It is a game between two players that is designed to see how one player reacts to another player's decision. The following is a good description of the scenarios the game provides. The choices for each move are to either cooperate or to defect, and depending on the combination of both players' decisions, points for the move are assigned to each player as follows:

If players A and B both defect, each gets 1 point

If player A defects, and player B cooperates, A receives 5 points, B receives 0

If player B defects, and player A cooperates, B receives 5 points, A receives 0

If players A and B both cooperate, each receives 3 points.

Unlike a zero-sum game (chess for instance) cooperation becomes the best solution. The problem is, for single moves, regardless of the decision of the other player, the best decision is to defect. It has been shown (Axelrod) that the best outcome of this game is for a player is to adopt a "tit for tat" strategy that begins with a cooperative move (this assumes a long term relationship is involved!) This can be applied to players involved in a symbiotic relationship such as entrepreneurs and venture capitalists! It is also very important in alliance forming for the standards setting process.

privacy. Due to the need to disclose data during transactions (unless for cash or smart card transactions), privacy can be compromised. An individual's Rights to Privacy is becoming more of an issue as businesses are increasingly able to gather data and use data for multiple purposes. With the internet, privacy issues are exacerbated, as data is not only captured more easily during transactions, but data gathering is not exclusive to transactions (sites can track your movements etc.).

The customer should better understand four things with respect to data tranfer:

1. How data is gathered?
2. What data is gathered?
3. When data is gathered?
4. How data is being used subsequent to gathering?

These issues (data gathering by cookies for example) and data usage (using data for own business, reselling data to gain additional revenue streams, combining data from multiple sources to create new sets of information) are increasingly unknown to customers. This uncertainty can lead customers to avoid transactions in the first place (and therefore compromize an individual's freedom). TRUSTe and similar organizations are evolving to help establish standards in data gathering and usage.

Junkbusters is a useful site to learn more about your privacy rights.

Aside from the need to offer data as part of a transaction, another issue with respect to privacy is the ability for "outsiders" to view data that was not intended for them (either data that is stored or in transit). Cryptography is the science that is designed to protect information from those with whom it is not intented.

privacy seal programs. Programs that certify a site owner complies with the site's proposed privacy policy.

private key. A single key that is used to encrypt and decrypt messages. Synonymous with symmetric key. Compare public key.

private label card. A credit card carrying the name of a retailer but actually issued and managed by a third party processor.

private network. A private, leased-line connection between two companies that physically links their individual computers or intranets.

profiling. Collecting and analyzing information that individuals have provided about themselves (see registration) and information about their online behavior (e.g. sites visited and content viewed), for the purpose of targeting marketing campaigns.

protocol. An established method of exchanging data over the Internet. The "must follow" regulations that govern the transmission and receipt of information across a data communications link. Languages that computers use to talk to each other. A set of standards that assures that different network products can work together. Any product using a given protocol should work with any other product using the same protocol. Examples of Internet protocols include: telnet, email, news and world wide Web.

proxy negotiation. The establishment of a secure communications link where the negotiating parties (i.e. hosts) are not the endpoints for which the security association negotiation is taking place. Proxy negotiation allows the identities of the end parties to remain hidden.

Proxy RADIUS Server. A RADIUS Server at the Point-of-Presence of an Internet Service Provider or Network Service Provider that is able to access a client organization's RADIUS server to obtain user information and enable authentication of users attempting to set up a Virtual Private Network for secure access to the organization's LAN over the Internet.

proxy servers. Servers that cache Web content in order to provide quicker access for users, when new requests are made for the same content.

PTAL. Payment Transaction Application Layer. An open standard developed in part by CommerceNet which allows merchants to accept any type of electronic payment over the Internet.

public key. One of a pair of mathematically related numeric keys, it is used to encrypt messages and is freely distributed to the public. Compare private key.

Public Switched Telephone Network. The nationwide and worldwide telephone systems accessible on-demand from telephones and modems. It includes individual dialup subscriber lines as well as high capacity circuits that are shared by multiple users on a first come first served basis. It does not include dedicated local and long distance lines (e.g. dedicated T-1) provided by telephone companies to large organizations, to Internet Service Providers, and Network Service Providers. Sometimes PSTN is used to mean only those facilities accessible by analog dial and to exclude ISDN.

publisher. The owner of a Web site that provides information, entertainment, software, or other content designed to attract and serve Internet users. Some publishers accept advertising and derive revenue from it.

(consumer) purchasing process. The purchasing process refers to the entire process a consumer will go through before making a purchase. A simple model follows:

1. Consumer Awareness (understands there is such a market/product)
2. Interest (consumer learns more about the value of the product)
3. Desire (consumer understands the need for the product)
4. Action (consumer makes a decision to purchase a product)

Depending on the stage of the purchasing process, the marketer will adopt different tactics to move the consumer to the next stage. The web is the only medium that is clearly useful at all stages of the process, simultaneously.

The Consumer Purchasing Process contrasts to the Business to Business Process that requires the following stages: Problem Recognition; General Need Description; Product Specification; Supplier Search; Proposal Solicitation; Supplier Selection; Order Routine Specification; Performance Review, and also requires many people involved in the decision making process.

pure play business. Pure Play Business refers to a business that was established for the web, but had no prior physical presence. Amazon.com is an example of a pure play business. This is in contrast to a Legacy Business, these businesses are the traditional businesses that are transforming to the web.

query. Synonymous with search expression, which is the key word on which search engines perform searches.

QuickTime. A type of video and sound playback format for computers. Developed by Apple Computer, the use of QuickTime has become so widespread that it has become a video standard.

RADIUS. Remote Authentication Dial-in User Service A public domain standard which defines the interfaces between a network access server, such as a firewall or a remote access server and a system which provides authentication, authorization, and accounting services. A RADIUS server is a system that provides these services and supports the standard RADIUS interfaces. RADIUS was originally developed by Livingston Enterprises. Also see an alternative to RADIUS called TACACS+.

RAL Refund Anticipation Loan. A very short term loan made by a bank to an electronic taxpayer once a tax return is filed and due to be repaid when the refund is received from the Internal Revenue Service. When the IRS receives the return it issues a DDI (Direct Deposit Indicator) number that assures the lending bank that the taxpayer has no other debt to the government. RALs were once viewed as extremely safe loans but fraudulent returns, filed specifically to obtain RALs, have forced banks to raise their fees or abandon making such loans altogether.

RAS. See remote access server.

rate card. Pricing information of various advertising options.

rational branding. An advertising strategy that substitutes an offer to help Web users in some way in exchange for their viewing an ad. Rational branding relies on the cognitive appeal of the specific help offered, not on a broad emotional appeal. For example, Web e-mail services such as Excite Mail, HotMail, or Yahoo! Mail give users a valuable service (an e-mail account and storage space for messages) in exchange for advertising on e-mail received and viewed by the user.

RDBMS (Relational Database Management System). A program that lets you create, update, and administer a relational database - a collection of data stored inside tables.

reach of communication. Reach refers to the number of people a communications can reach. TV typically has high reach, although cable programs are more focused and therefore the reach is more limited as the programs are more targeted. A salesperson typically has a reach of one at a time. Reach of communication is usually a trade-off with richness of communication. The web is the first medium that breaks this relationship, and allows for reach and richness simultaneously.

RealAudio. A software product from Progressive Networks Inc. which enables the creation of audio files on Web servers and delivery over the Internet to Web browsers.

RealNames. RealNames used to offer keywords as an alternate site address system. Anyone typing in the name of a company, product or brand in the Internet Explorer address bar was automatically redirected to the official Web site. This is usually because the company owning the brand name has registered their brand name as a keyword with RealNames. The service was shut down at the end of June, 2002.

reciprocal links. Exchange of direct links to and from a site.

recovery key. The key that is used to encrypt the key recovery field in a key recovery scheme. The recovery key is escrowed at a key recovery center or parts of the key are escrowed at multiple key recovery centers. A single recovery key may be used with all versions of a particular product or methodology (e.g. Capstone), with the specific organization using the key (e.g. customers using the Northern Telecom Entrust product), or with a specific key recovery center (e.g. TIS, RSA, IBM, and AT&T). The recovery key may be associated with either party to a communication.

rectangle ads. New Interactive Marketing Unit ad formats introduced by the Interactive Advertising Bureau (IAB) designed to enable marketers greater interactivity and creativity. Dimensions include large rectangle (336 x 280), medium rectangle (300 x 250 pixels), vertical rectangle (240 x 400), rectangle (180 x 150) and square pop-up (250 x 250).

referrer. The URL or site address from which a visitor came from.

registrar. An official Web domain name registration service.

registration. A Web site visitor's input of personal or business information into a form provided on the Web site. Registration allows the Web site owner to better understand viewers and customers, increases the likelihood of users returning to the site, and usually gains permission to send marketing messages to the visitor. (See opt-in and permission based marketing.) In return, the Web site owner may provide the registrant with access to restricted information (e.g. a research report), a Web site customized for the user, a free service (e.g. free E-mail), a discount on products or services, entry in a sweepstakes, or some other inducement to register. Users generally expect, and Web sites generally provide, a privacy statement describing how the information will be used.

registration service. A generally free service on the Internet which requires registration by the user, sometimes including detailed user information, in return for access to the service.

relationship manager. Bank representative assigned to your account once you've started to process large volumes of transactions. This person is your direct link to the bank.

relationship marketing. Relationship marketing, refers to the notion of marketing to a customer with the expectation of a long-term relationship. This removes the need to focus on each individual transaction needing to be profitable, but rather the relationship, over its lifetime, be profitable. Marketers are now able to segment their target markets to the individual consumer (one-to-one marketing) and understand the value each consumer can bring to the relationship (life time value of the customer). Relationship marketing also focuses on customer share, versus market share. The share of the customer dollar, rather than the number of customers within the market. Relationships between the buyer and the seller are also likely to incur lower transaction costs.

relevance feedback. Documents retrieved in a search that are used to further refine the search.

Remote Access. The ability of individual PC's or branch office LANs to establish data communications with their organization's backbone network, usually over dialup links. Remote access is most important for supporting mobile laptop users and enabling telecommuting. Organizations may lower their remote access administrative burden and telecommunication costs by contracting with an Internet Service Provider to receive dial-up calls at local POPs and route the calls over the network to the enterprise network.

Remote Access Concentrator. A large remote access server often used by an Internet Service Provider.

Remote Access Server. A system which receives data calls, generally over telephone company dialup lines, and connects them to an enterprise backbone network.

repeat visitor. A visitor to a Web site who has visited the site previously. Repeat visitors are usually identified by a cookie that was placed on their machine when they visited the site before. They may also be identified if they registered previously on the site and must identify themselves at the start of each visit in order to access content on the site. Repeat visitors are often tracked in the log file.

replay attack. An attempt to break security by retransmitting information that was originally communicated legitimately. See active attack, one-time password system, and passive attack.

response time. The amount of time a server requires to process one request.

retail card. A credit card issued by a retailer, most commonly a department store, which generally requires no annual fee from the user. Unlike major bank cards which are intended to earn a profit for the issuing bank, retail cards operations are expected to lose money or breakeven since their value to the retailer is in encouraging customer loyalty.

return code (success code, fail code). A Web log file records whether a request to the Web server for delivery of data was successful or not, and why.

Possible "Success" codes are:

200 = Success: OK
201 = Success: Created

202 = Success: Accepted
203 = Success: Partial Information
204 = Success: No Response
300 = Success: Redirected
301 = Success: Moved
302 = Success: Found
303 = Success: New Method
304 = Success: Not Modified

Possible "Failed" codes are:

400 = Failed: Bad Request
401 = Failed: Unauthorized
402 = Failed: Payment Required
403 = Failed: Forbidden
404 = Failed: Not Found
500 = Failed: Internal Error
501 = Failed: Not Implemented
502 = Failed: Overloaded Temporarily
503 = Failed: Gateway Timeout

reverse pricing model. Reverse Pricing Model refers to a model that allows the consumer to establish his/her requirements and offer those requirements for bid by the seller. Thus rather than the seller marketing a product to the buyer, the *reverse* is occurring. Priceline has pioneered this model in the consumer marketplace, using airline tickets as the product. This model further reflects the changing power in the market from the supplier to the consumer. When this model can be effectively combined with the group buying model one can envision powerful groups of buyers creating interesting demands on companies.

RFC (Request for Comments). The documents that contain the standards and other information for the TCP/IP protocols and the Internet in general. They can be found at several sites through anonymous FTP.

RFC 1827. An RFC which defines a standard method for IP data encryption as well as the encapsulating security payload. (See ESP.)

rich media. Rich media refers to media on the web that offers an enhanced, interactive experience. VRML for 3 D, Macromedia Flash and Shockwave would be good examples of languages for rich media. The Rich Media SIG is a good resource for emerging technologies. Rich media is often used for banner advertisements, for homepage's and for e-mail communications. It is important, however, for designers considering the use of rich media, to understand the audience they are designing for, and make sure the audience has access to the information being conveyed via the rich media (browsers do not have many rich media technologies built into their viewing capabilities, therefore plug-ins are required). Many successful e-commerce web-sites, like Amazon.com, avoid rich media, and use a lowest common denominator design strategy.

richness of communication. The richness of communication refers to the depth and interactivity of the communication. The ability to use multimedia to present compelling information to the consumer.

While a TV commercial may be able to take advantage of audio, visual and text, it can only present a generic presentation to a broad audience, this is therefore not tailored to the individual consumer. Moreover, the TV is not interactive, further limiting the richness of the communication as the consumer cannot transact with the marketer. A sales person can develop a very rich presentation, based on the specific needs of the individual customer. The sales person can also execute a transaction during the presentation. This is a very rich medium. The web is also a very rich medium, as it is able to take advantage of multimedia, present information based on the individual and execute transactions. Richness of communication is usually a trade-off with reach of communication. The web is the first medium that breaks this relationship, and allows for reach and richness simultaneously.

ripper. Software that stores music in digital format on a computer.

ripping. The act of extracting a track from a music CD and storing it in digital format on a computer.

Robots meta tag. Allows you to instruct search engine robots whether or not it can index or archive a page, or crawl the links found.

Robots.txt file. Allows you to instruct search engine robots not to crawl or index certain pages, directories, or file on your server.

ROI (Return On Investment). The bottom line on how successful a marketing campaign was in terms of returns for the money spent.

RON (Run Of Network). Ads that are run on some or all ad space across a network of sites.

ROS (Run Of Site). Ads that are run on most or all ad space across a single Web site.

root certificate authority. The highest level certificate authority in a certificate hierarchy. In the PEM model the root authority is referred to as the Internet PCA Registration Authority.

router. A computer that determines the best way for data packets to move forward to their destination.

routing. The process of locating the most efficient or effective pathway through a network to a destination computer.

Routing is commonly handled by the network or communication software.

routing algorithm. The program used by a router to determine the best path for data packets to travel.

RSA (Rivest, Shamir, Adleman Public Key Encryption). A patented public key (also called dual-key or asymmetric) data encryption scheme that can provide both encryption and authentication.

run of category. The purchase of a given number of impressions from an ad network on a defined set of Web sites that have some similarity in their content or in the demographics of their customers. See run of network.

run of network. The purchase of a given number of impressions on an ad network without any constraints on which Web sites the advertisements appear on. Run of network purchases are generally less expensive than run of category or purchases on a specific Web site because the placements are not targeted specifically to the advertiser's customers (See targeting) and because the ad network has greater flexibility in placing the ads.

run of site. The purchase of a given number of impressions on a Web site without any constraints on which pages the advertisement appears. See run of network.

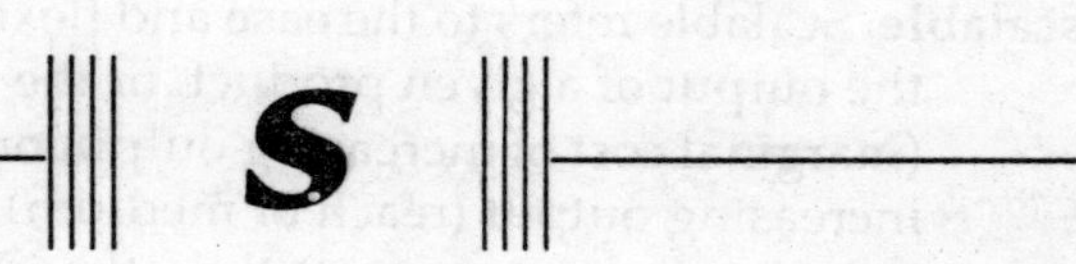

S-CDMA. See Synchronous Code Division Multiple Access.

S/KEY. A one-time password system released and trademarked by Bellcore.

S/MIME. Secure/Multipurpose Internet Mail Extensions. A specification designed to enable encrypted messages to be exchanged between e-mail applications from different vendors. S/MIME is based on the Internet MIME standard (RFC 1521). Some vendors endorsing S/MIME are: Microsoft, Lotus, QUALCOMM, and RSA Data Security.

S/WAN. A standard developed by RSA Data Security and several firewall vendors to ensure interoperability between competing firewall products. The standard will permit fully encrypted virtual private networks to operate between firewalls which encrypt at the IP level and which comply with the standard.

SA. See Security Association.

Satisficing. Satisficing is a cross between "satisfying" and "sufficing". It refers to the fact that when human beings are presented with numerous choices, we usually select the first reasonable option, rather than the best option available.

save area. The location on a computer where programs store critical information before control of that information is passed to another program.

scalable. Scalable refers to the ease and flexibility of increasing the output of a given product, or the reach of a medium (marginal cost of increasing output or reach). The cost of increasing output (reach of medium) by one unit. If this is insignificant (or zero!) then the product/medium is highly scalable. The web and digital products are highly scalable.

scalability. The ability of a computer application or product (hardware or software) to continue to function well as it (or its context) is changed in size or volume in order to meet a user need.

Scooter. The name of AltaVista's search engine spider.

screensavers. Programs or animated images that are activated on a personal computer display when no user activity has been sensed for a certain time.

scrip. A paper receipt dispensed by a scrip terminal that substitutes for cash in a retail establishment. Usually the scrip must be used at a specific retailer within twenty-four hours.

scrip terminal. Similar to a small ATM terminal and used with an ATM or debit card to access an ATM network, a scrip terminal issues scrip which may be used to purchase goods or be exchanged for cash at a specific retailer. Located in stores, scrip terminals are less expensive to install and maintain than an ATM terminal because they do not need to protect cash.

script. A record of keystrokes and commands that can be played back in order to automate routing tasks, such as logging on to an online service.

SCSI (Small Computer System Interface). A method of linking up to 8 disk drives or other devices to a single PC, MAC or other computer workstation.

SDSI Simple Distributed Security Infrastructure. An alternative to the X.509 standard for digital certificates which uses a simple human-understandable language. In SDSI language certificates are signed statements and the digital signature is appended to the list that forms the statement. SDSI is being developed by Microsoft and MIT.

SDV. Switched digital video. Network technology which carries digital video signals over fiber optic cables and is intended to provide the backbone for delivering services such as Video on Demand to households.

search engine. Search engines are web sites that are designed to allow you to search across the web. Each typically has about 30% of the web cataloged in its database (one reason for large descrepancies in search results). Search engines are a type of infomediary. Popular search engines include: Google, Yahoo, Altavista, and Excite. Other search engines that are emerging include: Overture.com and the Open Directory Project. Search engines rely on web deisgners to submit their pages to the engine, and on a spider that crawls the web to identify new sites.

Search engines are a popular source of advertising space. Since people are using search engines to seek out information and go elsewhere on the web, this fits with hypertext advertisements. Emerging search engine advertising programs include Google Adwords and Overture. These are CPC advertising programs that host text advertisements.

search engine optimization (SEO)/positioning/placement. An Internet marketing concept whereby you improve your Web site's design and content to achieve higher rankings in search engines.

search engine rankings. A measure of a Web site's visibility in the search engines.

search engine submissions/registration. The act of registering a site with the search engines, so that it is searchable by search engine users.

search expression. The key word on which search engines perform searches, which can include instructions telling the search engine how to perform its search.

search term/phrase. Word or phrase that people enter into search engine and Web directory search forms.

Section 508. A federal mandate requiring that information technology be made accessible to people with disabilities. Much of Section 508 compliance concerns making Web sites, intranets, and web-enabled applications accessible.

secure container. A technology which uses encryption to ensure that a content provider receives payment each time a customer views a document or piece of data.

Secure Courier. A protocol developed by Netscape which encrypts portions of online bank card and micropayment transactions in "secure digital envelopes" so that they can be sent by consumers to financial institutions without being understood by intermediaries (e.g. merchants) or by unauthorized parties. The protocol is based on SSL and provides functionality similar to CyberCash.

secured credit card. A credit card issued to a person with a poor credit record where the credit limit on the account is equal to the amount of money the person has deposited at the issuing bank.

secure electronic transaction (SET). A secure protocol that provides security for card payments as the traverse the Internet between merchant sites and processing banks.

secure envelope. A security utility that encapsulates a message and provides secrecy, integrity, and client/server authentication.

secure servers. Web servers that use encryption technology to prevent non-authorized users from intercepting and reading sensitive messages sent via the Internet.

SecureWeb. A software developer's toolkit from Terisa Systems which merges Secure Sockets Layer (SSL) and S-HTTP into a single solution.

Security Association (SA). The combination of a policy and a key used to establish a secure and authenticated channel between two hosts. The ISAKMP SA is the shared policy and key used by the negotiating peers in the ISAKMP protocol to protect their communication.

security gateway. A system which acts as the communications gateway between external untrusted systems and trusted hosts on their own subnetwork . It provides security services for the trusted hosts when they communicate with external untrusted systems. When a security gateway is providing services on behalf of one or more hosts on a trusted subnet, the security gateway establishes the Security Association on behalf of its trusted host and provides security services between the security gateway and the external systems. In this case, the gateway uses the IP Authentication Header, while all of the systems behind the gateway on the trusted subnet may take advantage of IP Authentication Header services without having to implement them.

security kernel. The hardware or software that provides security functions for a computer system. See information security.

seigniorage. In economics, the income a government receives from the minting of currency (coins and paper bills) derived from the difference between the cost of materials in the currency and the currency's face value. US government annual income from seigniorage approaches twenty billion dollars. Digital cash, issued by banks or other parties, may be opposed by governments because it can replace currency and decrease government income from seigniorage.

self hosting. A system of Web hosting in which the online business owns and maintains the server and all its software.

sell through rate. Percentage of ad inventory sold, excluding traded or bartered inventory.

SEPP. Secure Electronic Payment Protocol. A MasterCard network payment protocol developed and supported by IBM, Netscape, GTE, and others.

server. (1) A computer that hosts and delivers information to those accessing the Internet or an internal intranet. (2) A computer or computer application that delivers or routes information to other computers on a network (mail servers, Web servers, and database servers for example). (3) A computer or device on a network that manages network resources (file server, print server, etc.).

server error. An error occurring on the server. See return code.

server push. The continuous sending of new text, images, and other information from a Web server to a Web browser. Server push uses MIME's ability to send multiple documents within a single message to compose never ending message customized to an individual user's workstation. Implementations of server push, such as that from PointCast, are generally referred to as Webcasting or netcasting.

server side include (SSI). A type of HTML comment that directs the Web server to dynamically generate data for a Web page when it is requested.

service mark. A name, symbol, or device used by the provider of services to identify its services and distinguish them from services provided by and sold by others.

Service Provider (or Internet Service Provider, ISP). A business that provides connections to a part of the Internet.

session cookie. Temporary cookie placed into a computer's RAM for use during the user's visit to the Web site. When the user exits the site, the cookie is removed.

session key. A key used by an encryption algorithm to create cipher text from plain text during a single secure session.

SET Secure Electronic Transaction. A standard established by MasterCard and Visa for the secure use of credit, debit, and corporate purchasing cards over the Internet. Co-developers and supporters are Microsoft, CyberCash, GTE, IBM, and Netscape. Other supporters include RSA Data Security, Terisa Systems, and VeriSign. SET represents an evolution, merging, and replacement of S-HTTP and SSL.

settlement. Process by which a merchant and a cardholder exchange financial data resulting from a transaction.

SFA (Sales Force Automation). SFA is a means of increasing your sales team's efficiency and effectiveness using technology to help automate, organize and track the sales process.

shared hosting. A Web hosting arrangement in which a corporate Web site is on a server that hosts other Web sites simultaneously and is controlled by a third-party service provider.

shareware. Software that is distributed free, on a trial basis, with the understanding that the user pays a fee if they decide to keep using it. Sometimes shareware programs are 'lite' versions of a program with certain functions disabled as an enticement to buy the complete version of the program.

shell account. An entry-level Internet access account. Instead of linking your computer directly to the Internet, you use your modem to dial in to an Internet-connect host computer operated by an Internet service provider (ISP).

Shockwave. Macromedia's Shockwave is a program for viewing interactive media on the Web.

shopping cart. An electronic commerce utility that keeps track of selected items for purchase and automates the purchasing process.

shopping cart technology. Shopping Cart Technology provides turnkey solutions for e-tail sites. These solutions include web site connectivity with a product database, capability for users to "store" purchase intent before the final transaction (this requires interaction with your cookie file) and payment processing.

shovelware. Text, graphics, and images taken from company marketing materials (e.g. printed brochures) and placed on Web pages with minimal adaptation to the unique characteristics of the Web as a medium.

signature file. The signature file (also known as the .sig file) is a file that can be incorporated into your e-mail such that each time you send an e-mail, the file is attached at the bottom. This can be considered as a replacement for the leaderhead of your company. It should include your contact information, and should be no longer than four lines (according to netiquette). It is considered poor netiquette to create a signature file that is greater than the length of the e-mail message!!

signed java applet. A java applet that contains an embedded digital signature from a trusted third party; it is proof of the identity of the applet's source.

signed message or code. A message or Web page that contains an attached digital certificate.

signed volume. Projected annual volume for a new merchant. This figure is used to track the risk of a particular merchant account.

Silicon Valley. Silicon Valley refers to the region of Northern California which serves as a hotbed for entrepreneurship. Hewlett Packard essentially served as the catalyst for this region, in the 1930s. It is the home for many notable high tech firms, a major part of the venture capital community and Stanford University. Due to the symbiotic relationships between entrepreneurship, venture capital and Stanford University, a robust ecosystem has evolved.

site map. A visual model of a Web site's content that allows the users to navigate through the site to find the information they are looking for. Typically, site maps are organized hierarchically, breaking down the Web site's information into increasingly specific subject areas.

site popularity. Refers to click through popularity, and how long visitors remain at the site after getting there.

site search. Searching of a single site.

SKEME. A key exchange technique which provides anonymity, repudiability, and quick key refreshment.

skin, skins. A "skin" is a digital, interchangeable cover (or face plate) used to alter the appearance of those MP3 and other multimedia players you open up and run on the computer screen. You can find all the "skins" you want at the following and other locations on the Web:

— Absolutely Free Mp3
— Winamp Skins at Team-MP3

SKIP (Simple Key Management for Internet Protocols). A key management protocol developed by Sun Microsystems that allows un-modified applications to utilize encryption and/or authentication to secure communications over IP networks. An Internet host can send an encrypted packet to another host without requiring a prior message exchange to set up a secure channel. Its advantages include absence of setup overhead and support for unidirectional IP and scalable multi-cast key distribution. SKIP's approach is burdened by the addition of an extra intermediate header of perhaps 20 to 28 bytes to every protected packet, which doubles the bandwidth overhead of protected traffic compared with ESP. Also see ISAKMP.

skyscraper ads. Tall online banner ads, usually displayed at the side of a page. Dimensions include Skyscraper (120 x 600) and wide skyscraper (160 x 600).

SLA (Service Level Agreement). The objectives committed to a merchant by the merchant account provider for delivery of services.

SLD (Second-Level Domain). The portion of an Internet address that identifies the specific and unique administrative owner associated with an IP address. The second-level domain name includes the TLD (top-level domain) name. For example, in ecommerce-dictionary.com, "ecommerce-dictionary" is a second-level domain. "ecommerce-dictionary.com" is a second-level domain name (and includes the top-level domain name of "com").

slotting fee. Fee charged by sites to advertisers for premium ad positions on their site.

SLIP (Serial Line Internet Protocol). One way computers can communicate with each other over the Internet (compare "PPP"). SLIP connections let you communicate directly with other computers on the network using TCP/IP connections.

Slurp. The name of the Inktomi search engine spider.

smart card. Smart Card refers to a card that includes an imbedded chip that can store data. Since smart cards can store data, they can be used in transactions that allow the consumer to remain anonymous (data storage with the consumer, not the company) which is a key benefit for those concerned with their privacy. Smart Cards have not reached full adoption at this point, (higher rate of adoption in Europe versus U.S.) The Smart Card Alliance is an alliance of industry leaders working for the widespread acceptance of Smart Card technology.

Smart Energy Network Alliance. A partnership, founded by Novell and UtiliCorp United Inc. and open to other companies, to develop and market applications that allow users to optimize their energy usage in real time. See NEST.

SMS. SMS refers to the standard adopted for text messaging via a cell phone. This allows people on separate networks to send text messages across networks. SMS supplements standards being developed for m-commerce.

SMTP (Simple Mail Transfer Protocol). Set of explicit steps that must be used by one Internet computer to connect to another computer to transmit a message to its next stop. The standard protocol on the Internet for transferring electronic mail messages.

sniffer. Software that detects user's browser capabilities, such as bandwidth, JavaScript, plugins and screen resolution.

sniffer program. A program that taps into the Internet and records information that passes through a router from the data's source to its destination.

SOHO (Small Office Home Office). A term used for the small office or home office environment.

SO Security Officer. A person appointed to manage some aspect of computer or network security (e.g. cryptographic keys).

social engineering. Within the context of computer security, the deception of a person or persons in order to obtain information one is not authorized to have (e.g. a password).

SOCKS. A proxy server software package that does not support caching but is relatively easy to install.

source code. The source code refers to the programming code that is written to develop the program, oftentimes it is compiled before it is run, therefore unviewable to the end user. Once the program is compiled, it is readable by a machine, but very difficult for a programmer to understand. All free software (open source) programs are distributed with the source code as well as the compiled object code.

One nice thing about writing web documents is you can see the source code for the page you are viewing. This allows you to more easily learn html. If you are using internet explorer to view this page, simply click on the *edit* option at the top of the page, then select *source*. A similar process works with netscape.

spam. Spam is the term used for unsolicited e-mail sent by marketers and individuals who typically have purchased an e-mail mailing list. The first major internet spam actually occured when two attorney's, Canter and Siegel, spammed usenet news groups with their green card lawyer offer. View EFF's Canter & Siegel Green Card Lottery Net. The problem with spam is it can make the communications vehicle, whether the e-mail inbox, the usenet newsgroup, or the web discussion board, useless, as it becomes difficult to identify good information from spam. Spam should not be confused with marketing messages you receive via a permission-based marketing program, where you have elected to receive information from a company. However, some companies are reasonably tricky in terms of how they use the opt-in option to get customers to give permission (often as one of the final steps of a transaction), so while permission is granted, the customer's intent to grant permission is not always there.

Spam can also refer to the notion of spamming a search engine. In this case, a marketer tries to gain multiple (and redundant) listings for its site on the search engine, by submitting multiple entries. The hope is to gain a high listing. Search engines claim to be able to remove spammers, this claim reduces the potential for spamming.

(web) spider. A spider (also known as a crawler) is used by a search engine to identify web pages in order to be cataloged in the database of the search engine (web site designers can also submit web pages to be cataloged in a search engine). Spiders therefore help search engines to keep up with the evolution of web content by crawling through the web seeking new sites. To control spiders in terms of cataloging a web site, a designer can include a robots.txt file that includes pages that cannot be cataloged.

SPKI (Simple Public Key Infrastructure). A less cumbersome alternative to the X.509 standard for digital certificates proposed by the IETF.

splash page. The first page, usually the home page, of a site used to capture the visitors attention for a short time as a promotion or lead-in to the proper home page.

SPM (Sales Process Management). SPM is the front-end evaluation and assessment of a company's sales process. Innovative diagnostics benchmark current processes, identify areas of improvement, and codify best sales practices. Through SPM, effective sales processes are put into place that enhance productivity and help generate and increase revenue.

sponsored feature listings. Paid text ads that are usually displayed at the top of a Web page, before the search results, in search engines.

sponsorship. The purchase of space on a Web page or other online document to advertise a product or service. The word sponsorship is often used to avoid the negative connotations of the word "advertising" and to connote the original non-commercial nature of the Internet.

spoofing. The fraudulent practice of masquerading as someone else, usually with malicious intent, and usually for profit or gain. To send email disguised as someone else, or as an established business when in fact you do not legally represent that business. To misrepresent a Web site as original when it is not. Compare name changing.

Sprinks. A pay per click advertising system, similar to pay per click search engines, such as Overture.

SQL (Structured Query Language). Pronounce it "see-quell" (not "S - Q - L") if you want to get any respect at all from programmers. A standardized language that is used to define and manipulate data in a database server. SQL is a standardized query language for requesting information from a database. The original version called SEQUEL (structured English query language) was designed by an IBM research center in 1974 and 1975. Oracle Corporation first introduced SQL as a commercial database system in 1979. SQL is used to extract specified data from a relational database.

SRI. A research institute, based in California, that runs the Network Information Systems Center.

SSI (Server-Side Include). A variable value that a server can include in an HTML file before it sends it to the browser.

SSL (Secure Sockets Layer). An open protocol for securing data communications across computer networks. The broad support for this protocol will promote interoperability between products from many organizations and will speed the growth of electronic commerce on the Internet and private TCP/IP networks.

standards. Standards are very important in order to establish a robust networked marketplace (A marketplace that relies on connectivity across consumers and multiple vendors etc.) If a market is fragmented with incompatible proprietary standards, it is not effective in serving all customers and businesses alike. Once a standard is established, the market may increase in size significantly.

The VCR market is an interesting example. In the early 1980s, two competing standards were evolving, Betamax and VHS. Betamax was considered the superior technology. For two standards to survive in the marketplace, either consumers would have to purchase two types of devices to view the videos, or filmakers would have to release their videos to both formats. Clearly either option is inefficient and creates additional costs to the market. VHS, a technology originally marketed by JVC was actually licensed to other vendors (alliance forming). This strategy enabled the technology to gain significant marketshare over a superior technology, but since Betamax was limited to only one platform, it was not able to survive. Once the tipping point was reached, and the positive cycle took effect, VHS became the standard, and Betamax disappeared (no videos, no VCR, negative cycle!)

Standards can be proprietary, owned by one company (or a group of companies), i.e. WINTEL and Frontpage. Standards can also be open, designed to increase the utility of the marketplace, where companies then compete within a larger marketplace. Examples of standards setting bodies in the open format include W3C (evolution of HTML) and Web3D (evolution of a 3D standard). In order to develop open standards, alliances across competiting firms need to form. Alliance formation is a political process, that involves aspects of game theory.

standard general markup language (SGML). A computer language used to mark up documents independent of any software application; it contains an international standard that defines methods for representing electronic documents. SGML is the basis for HTML.

static page. A Web page that displays unchanging information. Compare dynamic HTML.

STC Secure Transaction Channel. A patent-pending technology from V-One corporation which uses an "out of band" end-to-end security method with DES and RSA public key cryptography to conceal and transmit transaction data to credit card processors over the Internet. STC reduces the risk of merchant fraud by not allowing the merchant to view in plain text any of the financial data contained in the encrypted envelope sent by the purchaser. The data is decrypted at a decryption server used by the merchant bank or credit card processor. The U.S. Departments of State and Commerce have granted export approval to STC. See CyberWallet.

Stealth script. CGI script that switches page content depending on who or what is accessing the page.

stickiness. A measure of a user's loyalty to a site, measured in the amount of time spent over a given time period.

stock options. Stock Options are options, usually given to employees, to purchase stock in the company at a future date. The price of the option is established, thus if the company's stock price rises above the option price, the owner is able to take advantage of the stock increase (current stock price - established stock price). Options therefore work well for high growth companies and are used to increase loyalty of early stage employees. They are also used to replace some part of the salary which helps reduce the company's cash flow (burn rate). Stock options may vest over multiple periods of time. Thus a certain amount of the options become available at certain stages.

stock photography. Copyrighted photographic images that can be licensed for use in a Web site.

stop words. Common words and characters (a, an, and, but, he, her, his, i, in, it, of, on, or, she, the, etc.) ignored by some search engines to enhance the speed and relevancy of their search results.

STV. Sprint Telecommunications Venture. An alliance of Sprint (long distance), Teleport Communications Group (See CAP), Tele-communications Inc., Cox Communications, and Comcast (cable TV companies), which purchased the largest nationwide rights to Personal Communication Services for $2 billion. STV intends to provide a full set of services to both business and consumers, including wireline and wireless, and data, voice, and video.

subnetwork. An IP network in which a portion of the IP address is identical across all the devices connected to the subnetwork. A subnetwork is usually separated from other networks by a router or firewall. A trusted subnetwork contains hosts and routers that trust each other not to attack each other's security and trust that the underlying communications channel (e.g., an Ethernet) isn't being attacked.

subscription. The delivery of specific information to a user's computer. Users provide information about what information to deliver, amount of information, and schedule for updates. More specific than a channel.

subscription service. An online service, Web site, or other source of information and services which offers ongoing unrestricted access and use for a period of time for a fixed fee without regard to which particular information or services are utilized.

suffix. The three character end of a domain name (i.e. **.com**) used to identify the type of organization. See DNS and top-level domain.

sunk costs. Sunk costs refer to costs that are non-recoverable fixed costs. Digital products usually have significant sunk costs (when compared to other fixed costs) in the form of research & development and intellectual property (patents etc.) for the product. If the product is not successful in the marketplace, the costs associated with the the product development (intellectual property, labor) cannot be recovered. Thus when making pricing decisions about the product in the future, one should not factor in the sunk costs. If a product's cost structure is made up of sunk costs (no other fixed costs) and zero marginal costs then any price above zero will contribute to the company's bottom line. Other fixed costs, that are not sunk (rent, depreciation on equipment etc.) should be factored in when making pricing decisions in the future, since these are ongoing costs to the company. The company will continue to have to pay these costs in the future, this is not the case for sunk costs.

The development of the Netscape browser is a good example of a product whose cost structure was comprised primarily of sunk costs. Regardless of the success of the product in the market, the major parts of the costs were already expended (product development). This enabled Netscape tremendous flexibility as it used its web site to allow users to download the product for free (actually it was not free, but Netscape did not pursue individual consumers for sales revenue). The only type of cost this presented to Netscape was the opportunity costs of lost sales from those who downloaded the browser for free. These free downloads enabled Netscape to build market share quickly, thus establishing first mover advantage and significant market leadership (for a short time!)

Another example of a sunk cost is the cost of a seat on an airplane to the airline. The Cost of an airline seat is primarily fixed and sunk (as long as one assumes the flight was going to take place regardless of whether the seat was sold) with a small portion attributed to variable costs if one considers the food and beverage service. Thus it makes sense for the airline to develop a pricing structure designed to maximize the revenue of the aircraft during a flight. They can do this by changing their pricing depending on the demand for a particular flight, and by offering additional benefits to their frequent flyers (to upgrade etc. 'course I am writing this on an airplane!) Essentially, as long as the price of a seat covers the variable cost of the seat, its revenue will contribute to the bottom line of the airline. This assumes opportunity costs are not a factor.

super affiliates. Top earning affiliates, who are capable of generating a significant percentage of an affiliate program's revenue.

superstitials. Rich media ad format developed by Unicast that combines Flash or other animation technology with Java programming to deliver video-like Web commercials.

supply chain. Supply Chain refers to the distribution channel of a product, from its sourcing, to its delivery to the end consumer (also known as the value chain). The supply chain is typically comprised of multiple companies who are increasingly coordinating activities via an extranet.

surf. Another word for browsing the Web.

surround session. A concept whereby ads follow readers as they link from page to page, deploying ads from only one advertiser during the entire visit.

SVC. See Switched Virtual Circuit.

SWIFT Society for Worldwide Interbank Financial Telecommunication. A nonprofit organization that maintains a network for the international exchange of payment instructions between banks and other institutions. Payments between SWIFT member banks are handled over domestic funds clearing systems such as Fed Wire.

switched access. A network connection that can be created and eliminated as necessary.

Switched Virtual Circuit (SVC). A transmission media compatible with L2PT on top of which L2TP is directly encapsulated. SVC's are created as needed to support connectivity requirements between L2PT Access Concentrators and L2PT Network Servers.

switching costs. Switching Costs refer to the notion of the hidden costs a consumer is faced when switching from one product to another in the marketplace. Consumers should really try to factor in the switching costs when making purchasing decisions, since these impact purchasing decisions they may be faced with in the future (limiting freedom of choice). Switching costs are developed by companies in order to try to establish lock-in.

The airlines have a good understanding of switching costs consumers face, and have developed the frequent flyer program to raise switching costs and increase loyalty among their installed bases. Digital products can establish switching costs in a variety of ways, including user interfaces, user training, accumulated data storage etc.

symbiotic relationship. A symbiotic relationship is a relationship between two entities which is mutually beneficial for the participants of the relationship. Thus there is a positive-sum gain from cooperation. This is a term commonly used in biology to explain the relationship between two entities that need each other to survive and prosper. The bumblebee and the flower would be an example. The bumble bee extracts the flower's pollen for protein and its nectar for energy. The bumblebee, while collecting these sources, inadvertently brushes pollen from one flower to another to ensure the flower's reproduction process begins. The bumblebee needs the flower to survive, the flower needs the bumblebee to survive. These are positive sum relationships. Other relationships in biology, especially with respect to the food chain, are not so forgiving, being a zero sum relationship, where one player clearly benefits from the other (typically consumes the other). In this type of relationship, it is still essential that both players (as species not individuals) survive, or the dominant player will lose its food supply, and therefore die. If the foxes kill all the chickens, the foxes die as they lose their source of survival. If the predator kills all its prey, the predator will die.

One can see a symbiotic relationship between Venture Capitalists and Entrepreneurs. Venture Capitalists need early stage investment opportunities. These are provided by entrepreneurs. Entrepreneurs need investment capital to develop their ideas, these are provided by the Venture Capital community. Thus both industries benefit from each others participation, a positive sum game. It is important that each keeps this in perspective, as if one industry tried to exert additional pressure (prisoners dilemma!) then in the short term they may be better off, but the long term survival of the relationship would be put at risk if it meant that the other player may not survive.

SYN attack. A denial of service attack in which an overwhelming number of TCP connections is attempted on a particular network or server. The address from which SYN packets are sent is falsified so it cannot be traced.

Synchronous Code Division Multiple Access (S-CDMA). An enhancement to CDMA that achieves high channel capacity by synchronizing multiple subscriber end-stations to a central receiver.

systems administrator. A member of an electronic commerce team who understands the server hardware and software and is responsible for the system's reliable and secure operation.

T-1 leased line. High-speed digital lines that provide data communication speeds of 1.544 megabits (T-1) and 45 megabits (T-3) per second. Compare 56K and ISDN lines. A T-1 line actually consists of 24 individual channels, each of which supports 64Kbits per second. Each 64Kbit/second channel can be configured to carry voice or data traffic. Most telephone companies allow you to buy just some of these individual channels, known as *fractional T-1* access. See bandwidth.

T-3/T3. Digital line that can provide 44.736 million bits per second of bandwidth.

T&E card. See travel and entertainment card.

TACACS+. A standard which defines the interfaces between a network access server, such as a firewall or a remote access server and a system which provides authentication, authorization, and accounting services. A TACACS+ server is a system that provides these services and supports the standard TACACS+ interfaces. TACACS+ was largely developed by Cisco Systems. Also see an alternative to TACACS+ called RADIUS.

TACDFIPSFKMI. Technical Advisory Committee to Develop a Federal Information Processing Standard for Federal

Key Infrastructure A committee established by the Secretary of Commerce to develop guidelines and technical standards for key recovery. The committee consists of twenty-four private sector cryptography experts and is assisted by government advisors.

tag. A command in HTML, enclosed within the lesser than and greater than signs (<...>) which marks specified text as a heading, paragraph, list, etc. and for including images, forms which accept user input, and hypertext links within a document. Usually a start tag and end tag are paired around the content they refer to and form a "container". See element.

target audience. An audience group being targeted by an advertiser, usually in terms of demographics, interests, product purchase behavior, product usage or media usage.

targeting. The design of a Web site or of a marketing campaign (primarily the selection of Web sites in which advertisements are placed but also the content of the advertisements) to reach and to appeal to certain classes or types of customers. A typical consumer target market might be women, 20 to 35 years of age, with children, with household incomes over $50,000 per year, who work outside the home. A typical business target market might be persons responsible for telecommunications management in businesses with fewer than 100 employees. Some Web sites and advertising campaigns are targeted to groups with special interests (e.g. golfers, hotel managers). See demographics.

target marketing. Communicating with a specific group of consumers with similar characterstics, within a broader group of consumers who purchase the type of product. Market Segmentation is the process of target marketing. Once target market(s) are identified, the organization develops a product offering (marketing mix) that is positioned to be attractive to that segment.

t-commerce. Electronic commerce conducted via interactive TV.

TCP/IP (Transmission Control Protocol/Internet Protocol). A set of protocols used on the Internet. This includes SLIP and PPP. A language governing communication between all computers on the Internet. TCP / IP is a set of instructions that dictates how packets of information are sent across multiple networks. Also included is a built-in error-checking capability.

telephone banking. The provision of virtually all banking services over the phone. First Direct, a division of Midland Bank in the UK, is the world's leading telephone only bank with over 500,000 customers and no branches.

Telnet. Program that lets you access a remotely hosted computer, assuming you have permission to access it.

terminal emulation. A technique in which one computer imitates a terminal while communicating with another computer, such as a mainframe, by using special software.

text advertisements. Text advertisments are text links that are paid for by the sponsors of the target page of the advertisement. They are a form of advertisement that can be considered more contextual (assuming the text link is relevant to the subject of the web page), and less obtrusive than other forms of advertising on the web. Text advertisements can also be used for affiliate advertising and the emerging search engine advertising programs from Google Adwords and Overture.

text messaging. Text messaging refers to sending short text messages from a mobile phone to other mobile phone users using the SMS standard. This is becoming an increasingly popular form of communication outside of the United States. This is due to the economics of text messaging versus being online. Key advantages of text messaging (versus being online) include a user's ability to text people independent of computer access, rather than only being able to communicate when logged onto the internet, it's less intrusive than a phone call, and it is less expensive than a phone call. Text messaging is a form of asynchronous communication.

theme based content. A concept used by search engines to classify a site as one based around a theme, much like a human would.

thin client. The relatively low workload of a Web client, compared with that of a server.

third-party ad management. A service to advertisers that manages the buying and placement of advertisements on the Web and the analysis of the ads' effectiveness. Also see ad management service bureau.

third-party processor. A company which contracts with banks to perform some or all of the tasks necessary to process credit cards: authorizing and processing transactions for merchants, adding new cardholders, processing for cardholders, and collections. Third- party processors may be for profit or nonprofit. The largest in the United States is First Data Resources, Inc., a nonprofit third-party processor.

thrash or **thrashing.** To move wildly or violently, without accomplishing anything useful. Paging or swapping systems that are overloaded waste most of their time moving data into and out of core (rather than performing useful computation) and are therefore said to "thrash". Thrashing can also occur in a cache due to cache conflict or in a multiprocessor. Someone who keeps changing his mind (especially about what to work on next) is said to be thrashing. A person frantically trying to execute too many tasks at once (and not spending enough time on any single task) may also be described as thrashing.

thread. A message and its responses in a newsgroup. Together, threads form a conversation of sorts as people add responses, or they may start a new message, which, in turn, will have its own "thread" of responses.

threat. An act of object that poses a danger to assets.

throughput. The number of HTTP requests that a particular hardware and software combination can process in a unit of time.

thumbnail. A term used by graphic designers and photographers for a small image representation of a larger image.

tiered service. A combination of offerings which are priced at various levels. For example categories of information on a Web site may range from free to expensive depending on their value, timeliness, uniqueness, or other market factors. See subscription service and registration service.

timeout. An action that takes place after a certain time has elapsed. For example, your dial-up connection may "timeout" by disconnecting if no activity has taken place for some time.

timing attack. An attempt to break a cipher by measuring the time a computer takes to perform cryptographic operations.

tipping point. The tipping point is the point at which the growth of the company's installed base accelerates significantly. It occurs with products that are able to take advantage of viral marketing.

A tipping point can also refer to the nature of the market, and how its balance turns to favor one company over another. Thus once one company experiences a positive spiral from network effects, its competitor(s) will experience a negative spiral, and the market will have tipped to favor the market leader. This may lead to a winner takes all scenario, where the balance of the market clearly favors one company over all others.

title tag. The title tag (of HTML) refers to the element in the header that allows the developer to create a title for the document. This title is used for pages that link to the web page, including search engines and users' bookmarks / favorites list. The title needs to be very descriptive in order to encourage users to click-through to the webpage. The title should not be confused with heading tags within the page, they are viewed by the user on the page. The title does not actually appear on the page. The title tag can be considered similar to the subject header of an e-mail in terms of its utility and function.

TLD (Top-Level Domain). Identifies the most general part of the domain name in an Internet address. A TLD is either a generic top-level domain (gTLD), such as "com" for "commercial," "net" for "network," etc., or a country code top-level domain (ccTLD), such as "uk" for the United Kingdom.

tModel. What are tModels? In order for two or more pieces of software to be compatible with each other - that is, compatible enough to be able to exchange data for the purpose of achieving a desirable result - they must share some design goals and specifications in common. The registry information model that each UDDI site supports is based on this notion of shared specifications.

In the past, to build compatible software, two companies only had to agree to use the same specification, and then test their software. However, with UDDI, companies need a way to publish information about the specifications and versions of specifications that were used to design their advertised services. To accommodate the need to distinctly identify public specifications (or even private specifications shared only with select partners), information about the specifications themselves needs to be discoverable. This information about specifications - a classic metadata construct - is called a tModel within UDDI.

The tModel concept serves a useful purpose in discovering information about services that are exposed for broad use.

tn3270. A version of Telnet software that allows connection to IBM mainframes by emulating the widely used IBM 3270 family of terminals.

token ring. One of several combinations of electrical, packet-format, and procedural specifications used for transmitting information over a medium.

top-level domain. The suffix of a domain name is the top-level domain. A top-level domain is generic (.com, .edu, .net, .museum, .name, etc.) or a country code (.us, .uk, .de, .jp, etc.).

Trade Point Engine. An initiative by the United Nations to encourage the use of EDI between business partners dispersed around the globe.

trademark. A name, symbol, or device used by a manufacturers of goods to identify its goods and distinguish them from goods manufactured and sold by others.

traffic. Communication over a network and especially the *amount* of communication over a network. In network technology, traffic is usually measured in bits per second or packets per second. In Web-based marketing, traffic refers to the number of customer visits to a site or page measured in a variety of ways.

travel and entertainment card. A credit card, such as American Express or Diner's Club, which is oriented to business users, generally charges a higher annual fee than a bank card and provides a substantially higher credit limit. Though T&E cards earn less interest for their issuers than do bank cards they are generally more profitable because average transaction amounts are higher and credit losses are lower.

trick banners. Banner ads that attempt to trick people into clicking the banner, with graphics that look like actual links or buttons, or an operating system error message.

trojan horse. A program hidden inside another program or Web page that masks its true purpose (usually destructive).

trusted applet. A java applet that has full access to system resources on a client computer.

trusted network. A network that is within a firewall.

trusted operating system. The dominant security platform used by the Department of Defense and other high-security government agencies. It uses multilevel technology and contains privilege and authorization processes to control access to functions and commands. It provides an audit capability which records unsuccessful network connections, logins and logouts, use of privilege, and access violations. See CMW+.

TSTS. Transaction and Switching and Transport Services. A uniform set of transaction processing communications protocols using virtual private lines developed by Bell Communications Research.

TTAP. Trust Technology Assessment Program A joint effort of the National Institute of Standards and Technology (NIST) and the National Security Agency (NSA) to extend to the private sector standards supported by both for unclassified but sensitive systems.

tunneling. An architecture which enables the point-to-point transmission of electronic data in a format different from the format in which it originated and was ultimately received. Tunneling can be used to send non-IP protocols (e.g. IPX, AppleTalk) over an IP network such as the Internet. It can also be used to transmit unencrypted data over the transmission media in encrypted format without requiring encryption by the host or application at either end. The Point-to-Point Tunneling Protocol encapsulates the Point-to-Point Protocol for control purposes.

two-sided tags. HTML tags that require both an opening and a closing tag (<BODY> for example).

two-tier affiliate programs. Affiliate programs that pay affiliates on two levels. The first level pays commission for referrals by the affiliate. The second level usually pays a percentage of the business generated by sub-affiliates that the affiliate referred to the program.

U

UCD (User-Centered Design). A method for designing ease-of-use into the total user experience with products.

UDDI. Universal Description, Discovery & Integration (UDDI) registry is the name of a group of web-based registries that expose information about a business or other entity and its technical interfaces (or API's). These registries are run by multiple Operator Sites, and can be used by any business that wants to make their information available, as well as anyone that wants to find that information. By accessing any of the public UDDI Operator Sites, anyone can search for information about web services that are made available by or on behalf of a business. The benefit of having access to this information is to provide a mechanism that allows others to discover what technical programming interfaces are provided for interacting with a business for such purposes as electronic commerce, etc. The benefit to the individual business is increased exposure in an electronic commerce enabled world.

The information that a business can register includes several kinds of simple data that help others determine the answers to the questions "who, what, where and how". Simple information about a business - information such as name, business identifiers (D&B D-U-N-S Number®, etc.), and contact information answers the question "Who?". "What?" involves classification information that includes industry codes and product classifications, as well as descriptive information about the services that are available for electronic interchange. Answering he question "Where?" involves registering information about the URL or email address (or other address) through which each type of service is accessed . Finally, the question "How?" is answered by registering references to information about specifications that describe how a particular software package or technical interface functions. These references are called tModels in the UDDI documentation.

UDP (User Datagram Protocol). Another of the protocols on which the Internet is based.

UNCID Uniform Rules of Conduct for Interchange of Trade Data by Teletransmission. A set of voluntary guidelines published by the International Chamber of Commerce for the use of EDI and particularly EDIFACT.

unique page views. Unique Page Views refers to the number of unique users that access a page. This is determined by a combination of the IP address of the user accessing the page and the cookie file. Thus the unique page views metric is designed to calculate the number of individuals exposed to a page over a period of time, rather than the number of times the page is served, which is the number of impressions.

unique visitor. An individual who views a Web site during a specified period of time (e.g. a day, a month). A Web site's log file can approximate the number of unique visitors during a given period by using cookies to identify PC's which visit the site multiple times and using IP addresses to identify multiple visits from the same domain.

Unix. A computer operating system, originally developed at AT&T Bell Laboratories, that is compatible with a wide range of computer systems. *Ultrix, Solaris, AIX, HP/UX, BSD, Linux,* and *SystemV* are among its numerous descendants.

unmanaged hosting. A system of server hosting in which the customer is responsible for maintaining and staffing all servers.

untrusted network. A network that is outside a firewall.

untrusted applet. A java applet that is not known to be secure.

upload. To send or transmit a file from one computer to another (compare download).

upstream. The transfer of information from a client computer to another computer.

Uptime. The time during which a Web site is accessible. We use OpenACS's uptime monitoring system to monitor our Web sites. The OpenACS site can be a bit slow at times, but the service is free, so you can't really complain.

URL. URL (Universal Resource Locator) is the web address of a web page. Thus the URL for this document is http://www.udel.edu/alex/dictionary.html This is comprised of the domain name www.udel.edu, the directory alex and the filename dictionary.html Many times you will see a URL that ends with either the domain name or the subdirectory, this is achieved by using an index.html filename.

URL broker. A business that sells or auctions domain names that it believes others will find valuable.

URL redirection. The process of automatically redirecting a user to a different URL, without the user's intervention.

usability. The user-friendliness and ease-of-use of a product to achieve specified goals.

usability testing. The testing and evaluation of a company's Web site for ease of use by visitors.

USB (Universal Serial Bus). A daisy-chain serial bus used connect up to 63 peripherals to a single PC. USB is used to connect such devices as: backup tape drives, CD-ROM drives, digital telephones, joysticks, keyboards, mouses, printers, and digitized audio devices, memory card readers, i-Books and more.

Usenet newsgroups. Collection of user submitted messages and discussions on all kinds of topics that are posted to servers on a worldwide network.

user interface. User Interface refers to the intersection of the techical aspect of a system and its users. Users could be internal to the business / system (customer service support) or external to the business / system (customers). The design of the user interface typically has a significant impact on the performance of the system. Users of a system also learn how to use the system over time, so good usability can help to create lock-in to the business for the customer. A business' homepage is an example of a user interface, as is any other webpage hosted by the business.

username or user-ID. An address that designates a personal account on a large computer. For example, in the email address mrbill@oh-no.com, **mrbill** is the user-ID and **oh-no.com** is the domain name.

user session. Each time a site visitor with a unique IP address enters a Web site during a specified period of time; usually 20-30 minutes, is counted as one user session. If the visitor exits the site and reenters within the specified period of time, it does not count as another user session.

USMARC. A machine-readable cataloging record used by libraries. With millions of documents already indexed, a simplified version of USMARC is a candidate to become the dominant approach to metadata on the Internet.

UUCP (Unix-to-Unix Copy). Originally, a program that ran under the Unix operating system and allowed one Unix system to send files to another via dial-up phone lines. At present, the term generally is applied to the large international network that uses the UUCP protocol to pass news and electronic mail.

Uuencoding. A common Internet formatting standard for encoding files attached to electronic mail messages. See also MIME, Multipurpose Internet Mail Extensions.

V.32. A CCITT V series standard used by fax modems for half- or full-duplex transmission at speeds up to 9600bps over point-to-point leased circuits. This standard is worldwide.

V.32bis. A CCITT V series standard for modems transmitting at speeds up to 14,400 bps over leased or dial-up lines. This standard is worldwide.

V.34. A CCITT V series standard for full-duplex transmission at speeds up to 28,800bps. Modems adhering to this standard automatically adjust their speed to compensate for the quality of the phone line. This standard is worldwide.

V.42. A CCITT V series standard for regulating error-detection for high-speed modems. Modems conforming to this standard can be used over digital telephone networks, as opposed to the standard analog telephone networks. This standard is worldwide.

V.42bis. A CCITT V series standard for data compression that lets modems reach data transfer speeds of up to 34,000bps. This standard is worldwide.

value-added network (VAN). An independent company that provides connection and EDI transaction forwarding services to businesses engaged in EDI.

vanilla wafer. A cookie created by a browser that contains little or no personal information.

variable costs. Variable costs refer to the costs that are associated directly with the number of units of product that are produced. For example, the materials used in making a product are considered variable costs of a product. Each product requires X amount of material, the costs associated with that material is considered variable (X * number of units produced) since the total cost to the firm changes depending on the number of units produced. The more products produced, the greater the costs incurred. This is in contrast to fixed costs which are costs that are fixed over a number of units produced (factory rent etc.) Digital products typically have only a small portion of their costs structure as variable costs (when compared with traditional manufactured goods). These are typically costs associated with packaging and customer support. Break even analysis, which is a tool that determines the volume at which a company must sell a product in order to break even, distinguishes between fixed and variable costs in its calculations.

VBScript. A programming language that can create dynamic pages within HTML documents.

(marketing) vehicle. Vehicle refers to host that is used to carry an advertising message. Thus with the TV, a TV program (Seinfeld for example) would represent a particular vehicle, that attracts a specific target audience and is priced at a certain level. In the case of the web, websites that host banner advertisements can be considered vehicles (Wired, Yahoo etc.) Other business-related sites on the web are those focused on marketing and business transactions, rather than on developing compelling content that attracts an audience in order to sell advertising space.

venture capital. The Venture Capital (VC) Industry is a major source of funding for the entrepreneurial community. The industry itself has evolved over a number of years, but has only recently emerged as a popular career for many new MBAs. The industry focus is on early stage, pre-IPO funding opportunities. Typically a fund will be raised, that will be invested in a number of different opportunities, that are reasonably high risk. In return for the investment, the VC receives an equity stake in the business. The VC also helps the business develop its management team, and takes seats on the board of the company. VCs are typically interested in making few large investments, due to the manpower needed to support each investment (recruiting and board seats). They focus not only on the business opportunity that is presented to them, but closely on the management team that is offered (human capital is clearly becoming the differentiating advantage of any business at this point!) In order for an entrepreneur to have an audience with a VC, s/he needs to have a pre-existing connection (a reference to the VC). Without this, the VC is unlikely to review the business plan. This further supports the notion that the VC and entrepreneurial community in Silicon Valley is a ecosystem that benefits from the mutual relationships that are already established, and is resistent to outsiders looking in (almost a closed system!)

A recent growth of alternative sources of pre-IPO investment is coming from Angel Investors. These are typically successful entrepreneurs (cashed out) who are looking for additional investment opportunities in order to remain connected to the entrepreneuarial community.

Veronica (Very Easy Rodent-Oriented Netwide Index to Computer Archives). A program that lets users search "Gopherspace" by keyword.

vesting. Vesting refers to the ability to monetize the investment in stock options. Thus if your options are available in three years, they vest in three years.

viewer. See helper.

viral marketing. Is a marketing technique that takes advantage of a marketer's customers in promoting the product. This technique was pioneered by Hotmail. They launched their free web-based e-mail service with the tag line (at the bottom of each e-mail) "Get your free e-mail at Hotmail." As customers used this e-mail service, and were e-mailing others, they were effectively sending an advertisement for the product. This attracted new customers, who repeated the process. Once a critical mass of consumers were using Hotmail, the tipping point was reached, where the number of new users started to increase non-linearly. Hotmail soon became the fastest growing media company in history. Illustrations of its success include it being the leading provider of e-mail service in India, without having a physical presence in India.

Hotmail is a good illustration as it is a product that takes advantage of the connectivity of its customer-base and their connectivity to other potential customers. This external connectivity attracted new customers. The term viral marketing comes from biology and the notion of how a virus spreads. A virus spreads very slowly within its host, until it reaches a critical mass (tipping point,) at that point it spreads through the host quickly.

Multi-Level Marketing (MLM) has some similarities to viral marketing, in terms of taking advantage of the connectivity of customers with potential customers, but MLM offers a direct incentive for customers to recruit additional customers.

virtual bank. A bank that serves consumers over the Internet and through automated teller machines without establishing branch banks or any walk-in banking facilities.

virtual bank branch. A three dimensional representation on the Internet of a bank branch office which allows customers to obtain information and conduct many of the transactions possible at an actual branch bank. The Electronic Courtyard is an implementation of a virtual bank branch by Visa International and Worlds Inc. using a version of VRML (Virtual Reality Modeling Language).

virtual dialup. Dialup access to the Internet that supports the use of unregistered IP addresses and the use of multiple protocols. It allows users of many different protocols (e.g. IP, IPX, AppleTalk) to share common network access (particularly remote access) facilities such as modems, Network Access Servers and ISDN routers.

virtual domain. A Virtual Domain is a domain name which is associated with an IP address, but is not the primary domain name for that IP address. This is used by web hosting companies to provide web hosting services for web sites whose addresses are not part of the hosting company's domain. Therefore when selecting a web host provider, you are not limited to using their domain name as part of your URL. Use of virtual domains means that an individual server does not have to exist for each individual domain name.

virtual hosting. The provision of Web server hosting service so that an individual or company doesn't have to purchase and maintain its own Web server and connections to the Internet.

virtual POP. A point of presence that supports an Internet Service Provider's customers but is actually provided by a Network Service Provider. The ISP contracts with the NSP to provide the POP.

virtual private network (VPN). A network that uses public networks and their protocols to transmit sensitive data using a system called "tunneling" or "encapsulation".

virtual safe deposit box. A service that provides secure online storage of important or confidential electronic documents.

virtual servers. A server at someone else's location that is shared by multiple Web site owners, so that each owner can use and administer it as though they had complete control of the server.

virus. A virus, a term "borrowed" from biology, is a malicious program that inserts itself into other program files to cause damage to the files. A user can inadvertantly transfer infected files to other users using e-mail (infected files can also be transferred by other means).

A worm, as contrasted from a virus, is a self-replicating program that duplicates itself by means of the network, rather than an individual user taking (inadvertant) action.

A Trojan Horse, similar to a virus, infects a user's machine by "appearing" to be a useful program (electronic greeting card, screen saver etc.) that people willingly forward to others, unaware of the hidden maliciousness of the file.

visit. The act of accessing and viewing a World Wide Web site.

visitor. An individual who views a Web site. See visit and unique visitor.

VMS. The native operating system of Digital Equipment Corporation's VAX computers.

voice over IP. Technology that supports the transmission of voice over networks running the IP protocol, such as the

Internet, with sufficient speed and continuity to permit two-way conversations such as a telephone call. The voice quality is not as good as standard telephone calls placed over the Public Switched Telephone Network but the cost of calls using voice over IP is extremely low regardless of distance. See IP telephony.

vortals (vertical industry portals). Web sites that provide a gateway, or portal, to information related to a particular industry, such as automobile, health care, or insurance.

VPI Virtual Private Internet. A creation of TradeWave Corporation which sets up a private network running over the Internet by incorporating a security system that recognizes only a given company's offices and personnel as being on the network. VPI's can be extended to selected customers and suppliers. A VPI is less expensive to set up and operate than a private wide area network (WAN) or, for EDI, a value added network (VAN), but does not provide the audit trail and management information provided by a WAN or VAN.

VPL. Virtual Private Line. A telephone company service which appears to the customer to be a dedicated line but is provided at a lower cost than a true dedicated line because it actually switches traffic over shared circuits.

VSAT. Very small aperture satellite antenna. Earth-based satellite antennas generally less than 24 inches in diameter which are relatively inexpensive and are widely used by retailers for communicating credit card verification and other information to company headquarters.

VT100. The DEC terminal (actually, the terminal's operating parameters and command set) generally used to define the option of "standard computer terminal". Countless other terminals, as well as PC telecommunications programs, can emulate the VT100.

W

WAIS (Wide Area Information Servers). An Internet multimedia search-and-retrieve tool offering more than 500 databases. WAIS (pronounced "ways") lets users look through the full text of the document.

walled garden. An approach planned by cable TV companies to offer free access, through the TV screen and a remote control device, to a limited set of Web sites, pages, and services. The approach will support localization of the offered Web sites and will allow the cable operators to charge merchants for making their Web sites available through the free service. For unlimited access to the World Wide Web consumers will need to pay a fee.

WAP (Wireless Application Protocol). An open international standard for applications that use wireless communication. For example, e.g. Email and Internet access from a mobile phone.

WASP (Wireless Applications Service Provider). An organization that provides content and applications for wireless devices.

WAV (Wave file). A popular audio file format that has become a standard PC audio file format for everything from system and game sounds to CD-quality audio. Files in this format end in ".wav".

Web. As defined by John Hagel III of McKinsey & Company, a set of companies which collaborate around a particular technology, such as the Microsoft/Intel PC web, and the Web surrounding Netscape Internet software. Webs require a technological standard and increasing returns to scale but work without formal alliances. They spread risk, reduce complexity, and enhance an industry's overall ability to innovate.

web analytics. Also known as *Web traffic analysis*, it is a process that involves the parsing of a Web log file and the study of its contents to learn: **how many** and **what** pages were viewed, **who** visited the site, **where** they came from, **when** they entered, **how long** they stayed, **what** paths they took, and a whole lot more. WebTrends makes software that does just that *AND* produces detailed reports to help you learn more about your site and how it attracts customers. If you do business online, Web analytics is a fast and easy way to capture information, study your demographics, and make sound business decisions based on solid facts.

Web browsers. Programs that lets you view Web pages on the World Wide Web. Popular Web browsers are Microsoft's Internet Explorer and Netscape's Navigator.

Web catalog model. A business model of selling goods and services on the Web wherein the seller establishes a brand image that conveys quality and uses the strength of that image to sell through catalogs mailed to prospective buyers. Buyers place orders by mail or by calling the seller's toll-free telephone number.

Web client. A computer that is connected to the Internet and used to download Web pages.

WebCrawler. Metasearch engine powered by InfoSpace.

Web design. The design and development of a Web site.

Web directories. Searchable subject guides, typically organized by major topics and subtopics. The best-known directories are Yahoo!, the Open Directory Project (Dmoz.org) and LookSmart.

Web hosting. A business relationship that provides the Internet access services of an ISP along with electronic commerce software, store space, and commerce experts.

weblogs/blogs. Web pages usually made up of short, frequently updated posts (links, commentary, news, diaries, project updates, etc.) that are arranged chronologically.

Web mall. A type of Web hosting that groups commerce sites in a portal-style directory.

Web portal. A location on the Web that acts as a launching point for searching, navigating, and other Web-based activities.

Web Request Broker. Oracle's API for linking its WebServer to applications and databases. Web Request Broker bypasses the Common Gateway Interface. It enables a high-performance native connection to Oracle7 databases. Web Request Broker supports development languages such as Java, PL/SQL and C/C++, and provides an open API for building server objects to extend Oracle WebServer capabilities.

Web ring. Web ring refers to a "ring" of web sites which forms a common navigation to allow browsers to view each site within the ring. The rings are comprised of sites with a common interest, so it allows those sites to potentially broaden their audience by linking with each other. This is a form of free advertising, much like bartering and banner exchange programs. You can view WebRing to search current networks.

Web server. A computer that is connected to the Internet that stores files written in HTML that are publicly available through an Internet connection.

Web traffic. The number of visitors to a Web site over a given period of time.

WebTV. MSN TV, former know as WebTV, provides Web access via a standard television using a set-top modem box, similar to a cable TV box.

Web usability. The user-friendliness and ease-of-use of a Web site to achieve specified goals.

Web year. Like a dog year, a Web year is approximately one seventh of a calendar year. It refers to the period during which business practices on the Web evolve as much as practices in any other environment evolve in a standard year.

Web-based E-mail. A method of providing E-mail that requires a user to log into a Web site to send and retrieve E-mail, rather than using the domain name and mail server on the network the user's computer is connected to (frequently the domain name mail server of the user's Internet Service Provider). Mail messages are stored on the E-mail Web site, freeing up storage space on the user's hard disk. Web-based E-mail allows the user to easily access E-mail from any computer connected to the Internet, regardless of location or type of connection.

Web-wrap agreement. An agreement to abide by the terms of a license agreement signified by downloading the software to which the license agreement applies. If the license is not provided for review prior to the download the agreement is generally held to be unenforceable.

webcasting. The broadcasting of information over the Internet using server push technology. The most common form of netcasting.

Webertising. Advertising on the World Wide Web.

Weblet. A competitor to Java from Eolas Technologies which provides an interactive environment for Web applications written in Perl and Safe-Tcl/Tk.

WebSpace. A helper application from Silicon Graphics and Template Graphics which allows Web browsers to view three dimensional space modeled in VRML (Virtual Reality Modeling Language).

WebSTONE. Benchmarking software developed by Silicon Graphics for measuring the performance of Web servers responding to a variety of client requests (straight HTML, CGI, and proprietary API) and serving a variable number of simulated clients. WebSTONE initiates the client requests and measures throughput, connections per second, average response time, and error rate. It runs entirely on client workstations and can therefore be used to measure the performance of any Web server.

webtone. The concept of providing access to the World Wide Web with the availability, reliability, performance, and ease of access that are currently provided by the Public Switched Telephone Network and which are signified by dialtone.

WHOIS++. An Internet search architecture developed by Bunyip Information Systems which relies on a search protocol intended to be compatible with the X.500 directory service.

Windows CE. An operating system based on the Microsoft Windows operating system designed for mobile computers and devices.

winner takes all. The winner takes all phenomena, for digital marketplaces, highlights the notion that markets tend to favor the market leader to such an extent, other competitors can be driven out of the marketplace. This is a result of two issues. The network effects and positive spiral experienced by the market leader, making its product more compelling for the consumer, and the learning curve effect and reduced average costs of the market leader, enabling it to potentially reduce prices to a price point with which competitors cannot compete. Markets will tend to tip, and this is when the winner takes all phenomena comes into play.

Winsock application. Any program designed for use with Windows sockets.

wire transfer. Synonymous with electronic funds transfer, which is the electronic transfer of account exchange information over secure private communications networks.

worm. A virus that replicates itself on other computers.

word stemming. Concept used by some search engines to return search results that include keywords that extend beyond what you searched for.

WWW (World Wide Web). One of several different protocols on the Internet. The WWW is the place that people are raving about. It contains colorful graphics, video, sound bites, real audio, and much, much more. The World Wide Web (also known as WWW, W3, or the Web) is fast becoming the predominant tool for accessing and storing information on the Internet. Like gopher, it is a menu-based system. Unlike gopher, menu items are actually hypertext links which allow the user to jump among menu pages, directories, files, and documents, and other Internet (FTP, gopher, and Telnet) sites.

WYSIWYG (What You See Is What You Get). Web site editor or software program in which the screen displays what the end result will look like, while the document is being created or modified.

x2 technology or x2™. A transmission scheme developed by U.S. Robotics that is capable of achieving line speeds of up to 56 Kbps. This technology can take advantage of compression schemes such as V.42 bis, to further increase throughput.

X.435. A standard which enhances the ITU-TSS/ISO family of X.400 messaging protocols to better support electronic data interchange (EDI).

X9.17. An ANSI specification for private key encryption widely used by banks and government agencies.

X9.9 FIMAS. An ANSI standard for protecting electronic funds transfers. See FIMAS

xDSL. See Other Digital Subscriber Line.

Xenix. Microsoft Corporation's version of the Unix operating system.

XFDL. See Extensible Forms Description Language.

xlapse. The number of people who are denied access to the Internet at any one time multiplied by the number of hours service is denied (as in megalapse, gigalapse). The term was coined in 1996 by Bob Metcalfe, inventor of Ethernet, to measure an interruption in service so devastating it would destroy the public's trust in the Internet by the end of the year. Incidents occurring earlier in 1996 included Netcom's denial of service to 400,000 customers for thirteen hours and America Online's taking 6.2 million users down for nineteen hours.

XML (Extensible Markup Language). Relatively new language which provides more efficient data delivery over the web. XML is similar to HTML and both are used to describe the contents of a Web page or file.

Xmodem. A popular file-transfer protocol developed in 1977 by Ward Christiansen. The protocol works by sending blocks of data in 128-byte blocks from PC to PC. Included with this data is an error-detection system called a checksum. When the data is received, the error detection system ensures that the entire message reached its destination. If not, the receiving computer sends a request for retransmission of the data. Compare with Ymodem, Zmodem.

Xuppa. Xuppa, formerly known as Bay9 and Rocketlinks, is a popular pay per click search engine, processing some 125 million page views a month.

Ymodem. A file-transfer protocol similar to the enhanced 1K version of Xmodem. Ymodem also allows multiple file transmission, performs cyclical redundancy checks (CRC), and can reduce the file transfer size to compensate for a poor connection. Compare to Xmodem, Zmodem.

Yahoo!. A very popular Web portal offering all kinds of Web services. Contrary to popular belief, Yahoo! offers a searchable Web directory, as opposed to a traditional search engine.